ESCAPING
the Poverty Trap

Investing in Children
in Latin America

Edited by

Ricardo Morán

Special contributions by

Amartya K. Sen
Nobel Laureate in Economics

and

Gro Harlem Brundtland
Former Director-General, World Health Organization

Published by the Inter-American Development Bank
Distributed by The Johns Hopkins University Press

© 2003   Inter-American Development Bank
1300 New York Avenue, N.W.
Washington, D.C. 20577

Produced by the IDB Publications Section

To order this book, contact:
IDB Bookstore
Tel: 1-877-PUBS IDB/(202) 623-1753
Fax: (202) 623-1709
E-mail: *idb-books@iadb.org*
www.iadb.org/pub

**Cataloging-in-Publication data provided by the
Inter-American Development Bank
Felipe Herrera Library**

Escaping the poverty trap : investing in children in Latin America / edited by Ricardo Morán; special contributions by Amartya K. Sen and Gro Harlem Brundtland.

p. cm.
Includes bibliographical references.

1. Poor children—Latin America. 2. Poverty—Latin America. I. Morán, Ricardo. II. Sen, Amartya Kumar. III. Brundtland, Gro Harlem. IV. Inter-American Development Bank.

ISBN 1931003564   LCCN: 2003111122

362.7 E271-dc21

Contents

Acknowledgments

This volume brings together the contributions of the editor and six authors. Naturally, very special thanks go to them for their sterling inputs and no less for their responsiveness to the various editorial requests entailed in preparing this publication. In addition to these authors, whose biographical sketches appear in the section entitled About the Contributors, two consultants to the project, Stefan de Vylder and Pierre Frühling, provided helpful background material used in Part One.

The book is also the product of major contributions by many other individuals and institutions beyond the Inter-American Development Bank. Owing to limitations of space and memory, only some of them are recognized here.

Among the institutions, the following deserve special recognition. A consortium of Nordic agencies paid for the bulk of the costs of a seminar (*Breaking the Poverty Cycle: Investing in Early Childhood*) held in Paris as part of the 40th Annual Meeting of the IDB's Board of Governors, which motivated much of the work reflected in the papers included in the present collection. In particular, essays in Part Two are based on presentations given at the Paris seminar by Amartya Sen, Gro Harlem Brundtland, Miguel Urrutia, Robert G. Myers and Nancy Birdsall. Helge Semb and Marita

Andersson from the Norwegian Executive Director's office at the IDB were key to assembling the consortium and securing funding during planning for the seminar. The French government and UNICEF also provided welcome support for the seminar. Jennifer Haefeli and Peter Knight collaborated mightily in developing background material for the seminar that became the building blocks for this volume.

The Swedish government, through its Swedish International Development Agency, funded the work of Mssrs. de Vylder and Frühling, and the Norwegian government paid for a substantial portion of the layout and printing costs of this publication.

Many of the seminal ideas leading to this book, especially on the critical links between the intergenerational transmission of poverty and early child care and development, stem from the work of Harvey Leibenstein and Marcelo Selowsky in the 1960s on the root causes of poverty. They began to gel over 1997 to 1999 at seminars and other events sponsored by the human resources team of the World Bank and the Consultative Group on Early Child Care and Development. Mary Eming Young, who with Jacques van der Gaag spearheaded the World Bank's activities in this area, along with Bob Myers, who with Judith Evans co-chaired the Consultative Group at the time, deserve much credit for motivating the work leading to this volume. Young and Myers, in addition, have been close collaborators and guiding lights on a range of research, policy, and operational endeavors relating to our work at the IDB over the years on early childhood care and development.

Thanks are also due to *Cuadernos de Economía*, a journal of the *Instituto de Economía* of the *Pontificia Universidad Católica de Chile*, for permission to include, without systematically attributed quotes, selected and at times literal material from an article published in the special issue of August 2001. The article, *Escaping the Poverty Trap in Latin America: The Role of Family Factors*, was written by two of the three authors of the monograph on intergenerational transmission of poverty. It is also to be noted that the essays by Amartya Sen and Gro Harlem Brundtland were originally issued by the Sustainable Development Department of the IDB in 1999.

Part One of this book evolved from a study by the Social Development Division of the IDB's Sustainable Development Department. We would like to thank the following for their contributions: Carmiña Albertos, Paz Castillo, Ruthanne Deutsch, Andrew Morrison, Eduardo Rojas, Alfredo

Solari, Gabriela Vega, and Amanda Glassman, who also participated in coordinating the project. John Schmitt contributed original material for the study and Luisa Fernández and Jenifer Haefeli provided able research assistance. Detailed comments from Jere Behrman, Nancy Birdsall, Suzanne Duryea, Carol Graham, and Judith McGuire are gratefully acknowledged, and participants in two workshops provided useful discussion. Miguel Székely, Martín Cumpa, and Marianne Hilgert, of the IDB's Research Department helped greatly with use of the household survey database. Financial support from the Norwegian Women in Development Fund of the Inter-American Development Bank is gratefully acknowledged.

Mayra Buvinić, the IDB's Social Development Division chief, has been the driving force behind this publication. Her initiative produced this book, marshalling the financial and other resources needed to carry out the project, providing major intellectual input along the way, and otherwise motivating those who labored to bring it to completion. María Loreto Biehl was a most effective and cordial task manager in steering this project through the bureaucratic terrain, which often entailed coming up with imaginative ways of overcoming challenging turns along the way. Ana Filonov, while expertly typing and formatting earlier drafts of much of the book's contents, provided many useful editorial suggestions.

Foreword

About half of all Latin American children—48.2 percent, to be more precise—have experienced a developmental "failure" by the time they reach age 18. To reach this figure we added the cumulative percentages of those dying before the age of 5, those dropping out of school in three rising age groups from age 8 to age 15, and those unemployed and out of school between the ages of 17 and 18.

These are sobering statistics for a region that wants to compete in a global marketplace that rewards skilled workers over unskilled ones, but where inequality is pervasive, constrains growth, and is strongly linked to differential access to human capital (health and education) between the rich and the poor.

The region's future growth and well-being depend to a large extent on the implementation of policies that quickly and effectively reduce this percentage figure for development failure. In response, researchers and policymakers have paid increasing attention to demand as well as supply side issues in the design of education and health services for the poor and excluded. This volume contributes to these analyses by focusing attention on the family as a key lever to increase demand for these services (and, therefore, facilitate social mobility), or, failing this, to reproduce poverty and disadvantage. It highlights in particular the shortfalls in human development that often occur within the family during the early stages in the life cycle, bracketed by conception and the beginning of primary school. A clear message is that income is a fundamental but not the only constraint to a better future.

In other words, families matter.

The essays and lectures in this book stress as well the utility of a life-cycle perspective as a core element of intelligent social policy formulation, as well as the need for comprehensive interventions to combat the passing on of disadvantage and poverty between parents (especially mothers) and children. Throughout, the writings are rich in empirically sound ideas that can be used in the design of interventions to combat the intergenerational transmission of poverty.

The intergenerational transmission of poverty is a problem that begs the attention of all thoughtful persons in Latin America, especially those in a position to mobilize public opinion and resources to mount a well designed and vigorous response. The hope is that this volume inspires and helps shape effective strategies that, in the end, are neither as complicated nor expensive as others that the countries of Latin America have implemented in the past.

Carlos M. Jarque, Manager
Sustainable Development Department

About the Contributors

Enrique Aldaz-Carroll has a Ph.D. in Economics from the Institute of Development Studies at the University of Sussex. His academic and professional experience includes work with the Inter-American Development Bank, the United Nations and the World Bank. His expertise is in international trade, development economics and applied econometrics. Research work includes determinants of trade, trade integration, impact of education on trade, and determinants of intergenerational transmission of poverty in Latin America.

Nancy Birdsall is a senior associate and director of economic programs at the Carnegie Endowment for International Peace. From 1993 to 1998, she was the Executive Vice-President of the IDB. She previously held various policy and management positions at the World Bank, including director of the Policy Research Department. Ms. Birdsall has been a senior advisor to the Rockefeller Foundation and a consultant for the Asia Society and the United Nations Fund for Population Activities. She is a member of the board of the Population Council and the Overseas Development Council. She currently teaches at the Johns Hopkins University School of Advanced International Studies (SAIS). She is the author of numerous publications on labor markets, human resources, and other development issues such as income distribution and growth. Ms. Birdsall holds an M.A. in International Relations from the Johns Hopkins School of Advanced International Studies and a Ph.D. in Economics from Yale University.

Gro Harlem Brundtland was the Director-General of the World Health Organization until July 2003. She has held public office for more than 20 years, including 10 years as Prime Minister of Norway (1981, 1986-89, 1990-96), the first woman to hold this position. In 1974, Dr. Brundtland served as Minister of Environment. Before that, she worked at the Ministry of Health on children's health issues, including breastfeeding, cancer prevention, and other diseases. She also worked in the children's department of the National Hospital and the Oslo City Hospital, and became Director of Health Services for Oslo's schoolchildren. In 1983, the then UN Secretary-General invited her to establish and chair the World Commission on Environment and Development (the Brundtland Commission), which is best known for developing the broad political concept of sustainable development. Dr. Brundtland is a medical doctor and earned a Master of Public Health from Harvard University.

Tarcisio Castañeda has a Ph.D. in Economics from the University of Chicago. He has served as a consultant for the World Bank, USAID, the United Nations Development Programme, the Inter-American Development Bank and the governments of Colombia, Peru, Mexico and several Central American countries. He advised the Minister of Health in the design of the Colombian health sector reform and worked on information systems for its implementation. Since 1980, he has served as the senior economist for the Organization of American States, sector economist for the World Bank's Latin America Region, and senior economist for the World Bank's Technical Assistance Project for Central America. He was professor of economics at the University of Chile in Santiago and the Universidad de los Andes in Bogota, Colombia.

Amartya K. Sen is currently a Master of Trinity College in Cambridge, England. He received the Nobel Prize for Economics in 1998 for his contributions to welfare economics, which have furthered understanding of the economic mechanisms underlying famine and poverty. Prior to his appointment at Trinity College, he was the Lamont University Professor at Harvard University, where he was professor of economics and philosophy

(1987-98). He has been professor of economics at several other prestigious universities, including Oxford University (1977-87), the London School of Economics (1971-77), and Delhi University in India (1963-71). Mr. Sen has served as President of the Econometric Society, the Indian Economic Association, the American Economic Association, and the International Economic Association. He is a fellow of the British Academy and of the Econometric Society, as well as a foreign honorary member of the American Academy of Arts and Sciences. He has received honorary doctorates from major universities in North America, Europe and Asia, as well as several international awards for his work. A native of India, Dr. Sen studied at Presidency College in Calcutta and obtained his B.A. (1955) and Ph.D. (1959) degrees in economics from Trinity College. His research has covered a number of fields in economics and philosophy, including social choice theory, welfare economics, theory of measurement, development economics, moral and political philosophy, rationality of choice and behavior, and objectivity from positional perspectives.

Miguel Urrutia has been Governor of Colombia's Central Bank since 1993. He served previously on the bank's Board of Directors. He also was the executive director for five years of Fedesarrollo, a private non-profit research institution in Bogota. From 1985 to 1989, Mr. Urrutia was the manager of the IDB's Economic and Social Development Department.

Ricardo Morán until recently was a senior economist with the IDB's Sustainable Development Department. Prior to joining the Bank, he worked as an international economics consultant and economist at the World Bank (1971-92). From 1967 to 1971, he served as professor of economics at Catholic University in Chile. Mr. Morán's professional experience emphasizes policy and program work on human resource aspects of development, including labor markets, poverty and income distribution, population, health and nutrition, and education and training. Since 1995, his work has focused on child and youth development among disadvantaged groups in Latin America. He obtained his M.A. in Economics from the University of California, Berkeley.

Robert G. Myers worked for 14 years (1983-97) for the High/Scope Educational Research Foundation, where he served as co-coordinator of the Consultative Group on Early Childhood Care and Development, an inter-agency mechanism intended to improve early childhood programming in the developing world. From 1972 to 1983, Mr. Myers worked for the Ford Foundation, where he was project director of the Office for Latin America, responsible for developing, monitoring and evaluating grants in education and the social sciences. He worked for two years at the International Development Research Centre in Ottawa, Canada to create a mechanism for identifying gaps in research on pressing education problems in developing nations. From 1967 to 1972, Dr. Myers worked for the Comparative Education Center at the University of Chicago. He earned his Ph.D. in Economics of Education from the University of Chicago in 1967 and his Masters of Education from Stanford University in 1962.

Early Childhood Investment and the Intergenerational Transmission of Poverty

Intergenerational transmission of poverty (ITP) is the process by which poor parents pass on poverty and disadvantage to their children. ITP is the result of interplay between certain conditions that characterize the lives of most destitute families in Latin America and the Caribbean, and as such it is a root cause of persistent indigence in the region.

Intergenerational transmission of poverty negates equality of opportunities at birth, and in so doing impairs the basis for a fair society and for social stability. It erodes social cohesion and fuels violence and civil discontent—particularly worrisome in the context of Latin America's current economic stress. By severely diminishing opportunities for the children of the poor to build their human capital, ITP hobbles a country's future productivity and with that, its prospects for growth and development.

By perpetuating an underclass of families without effective access to sources of human capital and consequent earning power, ITP is a powerful force behind Latin America's emblematically unequal income distribution. Only about 20 percent of the children of poorly educated parents in the region complete secondary education (ECLAC, 1998). Yet, attaining at least that level of education is the bare minimum required for a young person from a disadvantaged background to have reasonable odds to find work that pays enough for a ticket out of poverty, much less develop the skills to participate in the "information revolution" that is sweeping Latin America and the key to moving ahead in the labor force of the 21st century.

Whether reckoned by monetary income or parental schooling (as a measure of earning capacity and child rearing capabilities), poverty in Latin America—combined with relatively high fertility among poor and underschooled women—results in large numbers of children at risk. By the mid-1990s, more than 42 million Latin American children under age nine lived in households whose head had not completed primary school, and some 37 million lived in households with income below the poverty line of $2 a day.[1] Furthermore, most of those children lived in households with both of those disadvantages. Sluggish economic growth since then suggests that those numbers may be considerably higher today. With prospects for rapid growth in the years ahead as elusive as ever, the problem does not seem likely to be soon resolved.

The main purpose of *Escaping the Poverty Trap* is to raise awareness about the dimensions of the problem of intergenerational transmission of poverty. In particular, the book targets those in and outside the region who are in a position to affect policies—including officials from the public sector and corporate and philanthropic spheres, as well as the media and civil society—and thus act as catalysts in fostering a more focused and robust response to the problem than what has been seen to date in the region.

The book provides a framework to guide the thinking of those looking to tackle the problem now, and its success will be measured by the extent to which it fosters the political will and consequent pursuit of effective policies that could decisively change the prospects of the next generation of children of the poor in Latin America. Such a turnaround would surely improve prospects for the successful and sustainable transformation of the countries of Latin America into more prosperous, fair and safe societies.

The book also looks at the dimensions and causes of intergenerational transmission of poverty in Latin America as well as possible remedies for it. The problem is examined from two interrelated and complementary perspectives.

---

[1] Estimates based on household survey data from the IDB Research Department's Social Information System, May 2000.

Part One examines the intergenerational transmission of poverty from a systemic viewpoint that brings together the interplay of the components that make up our understanding of how ITP typically plays out in Latin America. This section considers how such factors as the demographic structure of households, parental schooling and ethnicity, and secondary education opportunities for children interact to affect the extent to which poverty is transmitted. Part One finds that the earliest stages of human life—from conception to primary school age (6-8 years old)—are the most critical interval of the ITP cycle. This is when widespread shortfalls in meeting the child's minimum requirements for physical and emotional care—as well as psychological stimulation and nurturance—often lead to major and irreversible impairment of long-term human potential. These essential childhood requirements are grouped under the term "early childhood care and development" needs.

Meeting those care and development needs is paramount to investing in early childhood, a common theme of *Part Two*, in which, following a summary, distinguished leaders in the struggle for the human, social and economic development of the world's less fortunate reflect on the philosophical, political and other fundamental dimensions of early childhood investment (IDB, 1999a). The scope of such investment extends well beyond the *direct* provision of early childhood care and development services. In the socioeconomic and cultural context of poor families in Latin America, most early childhood interventions—such as protecting the child during the prenatal stage and feeding and caring for his or her many needs during the months and early years of life—will be provided by the mother, although grandmothers, older sisters and other family members may well be involved. Improving early childhood care and development for the offspring of the poor therefore requires *indirect* investments in the child's family, particularly those that improve child rearing skills and other forms of human capital among actual and potential mothers.

The first essay in Part Two by *Amartya K. Sen* examines investment in children in the context of the overall development process—that is, opening alternatives to people as part of the expansion of human freedom. The Nobel Laureate emphasizes, first, the direct and integral relationship between a person's childhood and adulthood, beginning with the elemental recognition that a minimum investment in early childhood is necessary for survival into adulthood, and moving to the expected quality of life of the surviving adult based on the amount and nature of the investment in (or "preparation" of) that person during childhood. Sen then points to the indirect effects of the investment in a child on others in society, and on society itself, in terms of the person's capabilities and corresponding actions as an adult, particularly in the economic, social and political spheres.

Gro Harlem Brundtland states clearly in the essay that follows that investing in early childhood means investing in poverty prevention, so the way to break the poverty cycle is to focus on children. She highlights the powerful complementarities inherent among cardinal dimensions of human development—health, nutrition, cognitive and social stimulation, and education—but notes that health and nutrition, in addition to their direct value to the child's well-being, are prerequisites if other investments in child development are to be of much use. A sick or hungry child is not a ready learner. Such complementarities, Brundtland argues, call for collaboration and partnerships among the diverse actors in the field of development, particularly specialized multilateral agencies, in tackling the problems of children in poverty in correspondingly complementary fashion.

Miguel Urrutia revisits the rationale for investing in early childhood. Whereas this topic is examined in Part One as paramount to the array of causal and strategic factors involved in the intergenerational transmission of poverty, Urrutia focuses on the importance of early childhood investment in terms of its impact on economic growth and equity in Latin America, with an emphasis on the Colombian experience.

Robert Myers looks at early childhood investment from a more specialized and operational perspective. He largely assumes that the case for investing in early childhood has been made, taking on instead the task of providing a framework for going about it in a sensible and cost-effective manner.

Also presupposing the justification for better and more investments in early childhood, *Nancy Birdsall* highlights the role of the state in marshaling the necessary resources. Birdsall looks at the issue in the context of Latin American societies renowned for skewed income distribution and inequality. Throughout the region, only a small segment of the population has access to quality social services and to ways to participate in decision-making processes in terms of the use and allocation of public resources. Creating a political constituency for early childhood development programs and empowering both providers and consumers are key steps, according to Birdsall, towards ensuring that states provide sufficient and sustained resources for "win-win" investments that are good for both equity and economic efficiency.

One

Intergenerational Transmission of Poverty

Summary

The notion that the children of disadvantaged parents tend to do less well in life than those from wealthier families is probably at least as old as Western civilization. There are allusions to it in the Old Testament, and more explicitly in the treatises of John Locke in the 17th century and Malthus' *Essay on the Principle of Population*, first published in 1798.

The approach taken here to examining the intergenerational transmission of poverty (ITP) is more proximately rooted in the theory of human capital, particularly as developed and extended to the context of poor households in low-income countries by Gary Becker and Gregg Lewis in their work beginning in the early 1970s, associated with the monikers of "new household economics" and the "child quantity-quality model." The study also borrows heavily from the intra-household distribution model associated notably with Amartya Sen's work in the 1980s and 1990s, from the life-course perspective model put forward by Frank Furstenberg and others in 1988, and from Robert Myers' writings on the conditions for successful human development during childhood, and the extent to which these conditions go unmet among the children of the poor.

Drawing on a review of recent literature and empirical work, Part One of this book examines the effects of family background on the intergenerational transmission of poverty in Latin America. The empirical results are based on a cross-section sample from 16 Latin American countries accounting for most of the region's population, as well as on a sample panel of families in Lima, Peru, interviewed in 1985 and again in 1994. The findings clearly show the need for changes in government policies and in the design of programs to induce and support a quantum increase in the human capital of undereducated households—and particularly in the human capital of the children living in those households. Only such an increase in human capital will enable those children to escape the poverty trap into which they were born as they grow into adulthood.

The ITP approach used here is based on two fundamental concepts. First, it emphasizes the preschool period of life, beginning with conception, as the critical stage when vulnerability to lifetime damage is greatest, but when there also is the greatest potential for cost-effective interventions to break out of that cycle of damage. The second emphasis is on insufficient education as the primal vector of poverty throughout the life cycle and across generations.

The ITP Model

A simplified formulation of the ITP model shown in the chart on the next page illustrates its assumptions on causative flows and the cyclical nature of the process. It also provides a framework for identifying when and where specific programmatic actions might be employed to break the transmission chain. To better convey its key features and to keep it simple, the chart (and to some extent, the broader model) focuses on factors that diminish the likelihood that the poor will overcome poverty within and between generations. There are two main caveats to be kept in mind, however.

First, there are almost always at least some opportunities for escaping the cycle of ITP, and we know that a sizeable proportion of Latin Americans born to extreme poverty manage to do so. A guiding purpose of our work is to identify the most effective ways to increase those success rates. The simplified model shown in the chart in effect refers only to those people born into the ITP cycle who, failing to escape from it, would complete the cycle and reset it for the next generation.

The second caveat is that, since the model focuses on the internal dynamics of the poverty cycle, it may seem that it blames the poor for their prob-

A Simplified View of the Intergenerational Transmission of Poverty

In the midst of typically harsh social, economic and cultural settings with inadequate social services, oversupplied labor markets for the unskilled, and meager cultural opportunities and successful role models, a host of formidable impediments characterizing the environments of families in poverty include . . .

Parents with little schooling and scant marketable skills ("functionally poor parents") . . .

. . . who begin childbearing early, without the means or parenting skills to provide for their children's developmental needs, often resulting in . . .

. . . generally socialize with out-of-school peer youth, often resulting in early childbearing and thus becoming . . .

. . . stunted children with impaired learning capacity . . .

. . . have a high propensity for dysfunctional and anti-social behavior, work at dead-end jobs (or live off illegal activities) and . . .

. . . frequently resulting in school failure (repetition, desertion) causing functional illiteracy and thus leading to . . .

. . . out-of-school and unskilled youth with scant marketable skills and poverty earnings (e.g. functional poverty), who . . .

lems. In other words, it might appear to cast poor people as the main actors in a process that leads to adverse consequences for themselves (they remain poor), their children (they do not develop fully, remain poor, etc.), and even society at large (as when adolescents in poverty behave antisocially). It is thus worth emphasizing that factors external to impoverished households and people—such as the lack of quality social services (clean water, sanitation, police protection, health care and, most importantly, good schools) as well as economic opportunities beyond hard work for subsistence wages—more often than not configure an environment so hostile to human development that it is quite astonishing that some people actually manage to overcome such formidable odds. While we fully recognize that these impediments exist and wholeheartedly agree with mainstream anti-poverty literature that advocates supply-side public policies to improve these conditions, the ITP model itself, for heuristic purposes, focuses on factors that are indeed largely endogenous to impoverished families.

Insufficient human capital, reckoned in terms of education or schooling, is the critical dimension of poverty in the ITP framework. Led by its "initial" block (upper left-hand corner), the chart depicts critical stages and attending adverse features in the life cycle of "typical" individuals born to parents lacking sufficient education to earn enough to put them beyond the pale of poverty.[1] Their insufficient education and income also limit the resources they can muster for their children's full mental and physical development, such as good pre- and post-natal health care, balanced nutrition, and the time and ability to read to them and otherwise nurture the child's mind. Thus, despite the circularity of the process, the model, in effect, assigns to insufficient education at all stages of the life cycle the predomi-

---

[1] From the perspective of the ITP framework, there are advantages to defining poverty in terms of individual or household human capital, reckoned by years of schooling, rather than by the more familiar income- or consumption-based metrics, which in any case are almost universally found to be highly correlated with schooling. First, more educated people and their households almost invariably tend to have higher incomes. For the purpose at hand, schooling is the preferred index mainly because it is a far better predictor of lifetime economic well-being than the often transitory and volatile patterns of income from one year to the next, especially among the poor. Schooling also is more closely associated with notions of opportunities, capabilities and cultural predispositions that feature prominently in modern concepts of poverty, especially beyond mainstream economics (see Lewis et al., 1979). Moreover, schooling attainment can be recalled more reliably than either income or consumption by household survey respondents, which is a decisive advantage for the empirical investigation of the model.

nant role in sustaining the process. Eliminate this factor, and the process collapses.

In the ITP framework used for this study, people are deemed to be either "(functionally) poor" or "not poor." As noted earlier, the operational definitions used for grouping households and individuals in the corresponding category are based on schooling attainment. Households are classified as "poor" if the head (i.e., the "parent") did not complete primary education at the first round of data collection. The "children" from the selected households are classified as "poor" if by the age of 24 (Lima sample) or 26 (16-country samples) they did not complete the secondary level. The rationale for this classification is that having reached these ages, these people are unlikely to complete their education, and without a secondary diploma they are unlikely to find and hold a job for long enough over their lives to allow for a permanent transition out of poverty. Loosely put, if the child of functionally poor parents graduates from secondary school by his or her mid-20s, the model records this as an escape (a "break") from ITP; otherwise, it records the person as a "hold" in the ITP process.

Findings

Parental schooling, number of siblings, family income, and attendance in a preschool program affect a child's chances of eventually completing secondary education. Other studies document the effects of the mother's health and nutrition, domestic violence, and teen pregnancy. The statistical results show that a child's chances of completing secondary education are positively and significantly affected by the mother's and father's education and family income. The number of siblings has a significantly negative effect on the child's educational prospects. The effects are similar across countries and hold even at low levels of parental education and household income, and they are consistently strong for parental education and number of siblings. This suggests that at least certain core features of policy strategies to combat ITP can be usefully incorporated into national programs across countries, although strategies naturally should also include features specific to national and local conditions.

The statistical analysis also included an additional factor, although suitable data were available only for Peru: the child's attendance in a preschool program. The results show a very strong positive effect of this factor on the child's secondary school completion prospects, after controlling for parental education, family income and number of siblings. This suggests that preschool programs could be a powerful component in ITP-oriented strategies.

Other family factors affecting school achievement, identified in earlier studies, are maternal health and nutrition (especially during the pre- and peri-natal interval), domestic violence, and teen motherhood. Although these factors could not be indexed for estimation in our study's multivariate statistical analysis, they are probably no less important than the others. In particular, teen motherhood in the vast majority of cases is, without a doubt, a formidable obstacle to poor girls' completing secondary school.

Policy Conclusions

While poverty reduction policies and programs normally emphasize the supply of education and other services, family factors driving the demand for these services warrant more attention. Policy debate on structural poverty reduction in the region has typically focused largely on children's education and, less so on health and nutrition. However, the focus has been on the supply side of investments in children—for example, expanding school places and, more recently, increasing educational quality. Although the significance of family background factors (commonly known as *socioeconomic status* or SES) in schooling outcomes has been well known and documented for decades, those factors have seldom been fully incorporated as strategic variables in policies and programs in most Latin American countries. Until fairly recently, the number of primary school places fell well short of the number of school-age children, an imbalance that remains large for secondary schools, so perhaps it is understandable that the focus has been on addressing supply constraints. However, the almost universal enrollment of children at the beginning of the school year indicates that insufficient school places may no longer be a critical obstacle.

The basic education problems that persist are high rates of repetition, desertion, and ultimately, school failure in primary and particularly secondary education among children from low SES families or, as identified in the framework used here, the children of undereducated parents. Moreover, such problems have probably worsened as a growing proportion of these disadvantaged and failure-prone children have found places to enroll in primary school in recent years. Together with these evolving patterns, the findings from the study presented here call for much greater emphasis on the demand side of basic education for the children of the poor and, more fundamentally, on family-related factors that influence early human capital formation, education outcomes, and hence, lifetime prospects for these children.

Effective programs to break the ITP cycle focus on the family, reinforcing the positive influences of parents on their children and minimizing negative ones. Program design should take into account the predictable stages in the life cycle of families. Family formation, and the rearing and schooling of children, together with correlated stages in parental labor force activity and resulting earnings, are crucial parts of this framework.

While family-focused anti-poverty programs must reflect local conditions, at the core they must supplement investments by parents in their children. The costs of providing poor children with the conditions to properly develop their physical and mental potential generally exceeds the earnings capacity of undereducated households, especially since such investments coincide with a low phase in the parental earnings cycle. This applies not only to the preschool years, but also through adolescence. Thus, in the absence of focused social intervention, the potential of most of these children remains unrealized.

Early childhood interventions that offer quality childcare and complementary services to otherwise help parents provide a healthy and nurturing environment for their young children are the leading edge of our strategy to break the poverty cycle. These components can be powerful and versatile instruments that simultaneously operate on two key links of the cycle. They give parents, especially mothers, the time to improve their skills or the occupational mobility to increase their earnings, and they can decisively improve the conditions for the mental and physical development of their children.

Programs effective to break the ITP cycle may require substantial subsidies and other incentives for families to send their children to school and sustain their attendance, at least through secondary school. Such programs would generally entail subsidized tuition and maintenance (school breakfast and lunch, textbooks and materials) to help poor families pay the direct costs of education. In cases of extreme poverty, cash transfers to the parents to compensate for the indirect costs of education, such as family income foregone from the labor of older children, can also play a crucial role.

Anti-Poverty Programs in Latin America

Innovative programs aimed at breaking the poverty cycle already exist in Latin America. Mexico's *Oportunidades* program (formerly known as *Progresa*) integrates education, health and nutrition services with incentive subsidies, including income support. Honduras' Family Allowance Program *(Programa de Asignación Familiar—PRAF)* integrates school attendance and preventive health with income support for participating poor families.

Both of these programs complement demand-side family incentives with significant improvements in the education and health services offered to the poor. Other innovative programs include agricultural vouchers for poor farmers for the purchase of modern inputs and technical assistance, conditional upon the family's participation in early childhood care programs, health check-ups and reproductive health and nutrition education programs, as well as school attendance by school-aged children.

Integrated ITP-oriented programs, especially the more comprehensive ones such as *Oportunidades*, are naturally much more costly on a per-household basis than typical stand-alone, one-type-service (e.g., primary school) social programs. Because no Latin American country has the fiscal capability to enroll all the families that want to participate in such integrated programs—especially if they encompass a significant cash transfer component—it is important to establish criteria to select those that would benefit the most. The particulars of such targeting criteria, and how well they are implemented, are crucial to a program's success. Fortunately, advances in information technology and experience with various targeting methods in several countries in the region can usefully guide the design and administration of this critical part of an effective ITP-oriented program.[2]

---

[2] See van de Walle (1998) for a discussion of the different forms of targeting and the costs and benefits involved.

Family Background and Intergenerational Poverty in Latin America

RICARDO MORÁN, TARSICIO CASTAÑEDA
AND ENRIQUE ALDAZ-CARROLL

As a starting point, the intergenerational transmission of poverty can be analyzed in terms of a stylized version of the child quantity-quality model introduced by Becker and Lewis (1973) and Becker (1991) within the context of the broader new household economics framework. In the model, families derive welfare both from the number and the quality of their children, with the latter a result of human capital investments in childhood, education, health and nutrition. These investments require parental time and effort at home and in the labor market, where money is obtained for purchasing other inputs in the marketplace. Additional inputs may be available as subsidized public services, particularly in health and education. For poor and undereducated households, such subsidized inputs result in more human capital for the children than would otherwise be the case. Parental and especially maternal time is split between childcare (together with related forms of "home production") and paid work, depending largely on labor market opportunities and the family's demographic composition.

This Beckerian model is useful in suggesting key variables and relations to examine in order to understand the dynamics of ITP in Latin America, analyze empirical data, and interpret statistical results. In this model, the transmission of poverty from one generation to the next is a result of parental investments in their children's human capital that are insufficient for them to reach lifetime income and consumption levels that would lift them out of poverty. The amount invested in each child depends crucially on the number of children in the family, household income, parental education (which affects aspirations and the productivity of the investments), the cost to parents of inputs into human capital, and labor market conditions, the household's social environment and other contextual factors that constrain family incomes, opportunities and aspirations. The flagship index of child quality (or human capital) in the Beckerian model is the effect of certain of these variables on children's education or, more precisely, schooling outcomes. The study makes the simplifying assumption that, for the children of undereducated households, the threshold of schooling attainment that critically determines their chances of overcoming lifetime poverty is whether they have completed secondary education by their mid-20s.

To supplement the Beckerian model, the empirical analysis employed here also draws on the intra-household distribution model and the life-course perspective model. The former model relates the intra-household allocation of resources—notably, parental time and income—to the child's schooling attainment. Parental time and resources devoted to a child are determined by the number of siblings, the gender of the child, and age relative to that of siblings (Sen, 1984).

The life-course perspective model (Furstenberg et al., 1988) holds that events and experiences early in life shape the behavior and educational performance of the adult, according to personal characteristics and socio-economic factors. This model emphasizes the key role of the family in shaping the intellectual and social development of the child, from early in life and into adulthood. Early childhood nurturing practices, intellectual stimulation and affection shape the child's intellectual development. Children learn social (and antisocial) patterns of behavior early in life from the family. These behaviors are then displayed at school and in the neighborhood. The model points to early childhood care and development, adolescent motherhood, domestic violence, and health as important factors in the analysis of a child's educational and economic performance in the future.

Our empirical analysis draws on complementary features of the three models. Specifically, it examines the effects on a child's educational attainment of the number of siblings, the education of the mother and the father, household income, adolescent motherhood, early child care, order of siblings, health, ethnicity, residence and violence.

Applying the Framework to Latin America

Previous Empirical Work

Although early studies of intergenerational economic mobility in the United States tended to show a weak correlation of income across generations, more recent work using larger longitudinal panels shows the correlation to be significant (Gottschalk, Mclanahan and Sandefur, 1994). Behrman and Taubman (1990) found the income correlation between father and son to be 0.58, and Solon (1992) found a correlation of 0.40. Warren and Hauser (1997) obtained intergenerational income correlations between 0.24 and 0.36 for men aged 25 to 34. These estimates may be considered lower bound values of plausible intergenerational income correlation in Latin American countries, where inequality of opportunities is far greater than in the United States.

Research in developed countries shows that family factors such as parents' education, number of siblings and family structure affect children's future performance and thus play an important role in ITP mechanism (Jencks et al., 1972; Gottschalk, Mclanahan and Sandefur, 1994).

The abundance of economic mobility studies in developed countries stands in contrast to the paucity of such studies on Latin America. Economic mobility studies in developing countries in general are still in their infancy owing to very limited availability of panel data.[3] Although there are some studies on mobility in Latin America,[4] to date there have been no suitable panel data available to carry out an ITP study. Urrutia's (1985) pioneering work using panel data to study socioeconomic mobility in Cali, Colombia provided important insights into differences between "winners and losers," but its scope did not include analysis of ITP determinants. More recently, ECLAC (1998) examined the intergenerational

---

[3] A review of mobility studies in developing countries can be found in Fields (1998).

[4] See the study by Buvinić et al. (1992) on Santiago, Chile; the study by Morley et al. (1998) on Colombia; and the study by Glewwe (1995) of relative mobility in Peru.

transmission of education, using cross-sectional data for nine Latin American countries. But the study did not include econometric analysis of its determinants.

Statistical Analysis

The statistical analysis focuses on the effect of family factors on a child's educational attainment as a proxy for judging whether the individual will escape poverty, while controlling for as many other relevant variables as possible. A child is considered to have been born poor if the head of the household has not completed primary education. It is assumed that an individual born in poverty who has not completed secondary education by his or her early 20s will never complete it. Those completing secondary schooling are assumed to improve their lifetime earnings sufficiently to escape long-term poverty and the ITP cycle.

This human capital-based definition of household poverty is preferred over an income-based (or consumption-based) definition because schooling attainment can be recalled more reliably than either income or consumption by household survey respondents and, especially, because it is a far better predictor of lifetime economic well-being. In addition, it is also superior in this context because parental education is likely to be more closely associated with hard to measure features of "the culture of poverty" that have been found to affect children's performance in school (Lewis, 1979; Furstenberg, 1998).

These educational thresholds coincide with those used in the ECLAC (1998) study. The lower educational threshold for parents is also consonant with the close associations between notions of "the poor" and "the undereducated" found copiously in the economic and sociological literature, such as the references cited above. The choice of the secondary education completion threshold for individuals now in their 20s is based on the intuition that it will be increasingly unlikely for them to earn enough to live above poverty over the remainder of their lives without at least secondary schooling.

Since the main thrust of this study relies heavily on this intuition, it deserves further girding. First, we believe that the information revolution spreading across the region is driving increasingly education-biased labor demand, especially in "modern sector" labor markets associated with nonpoverty wages. Even for entry-level positions, job applicants are routinely expected to fill out various forms requiring a measure of information-processing skills rarely acquired in the primary schools that serve the poor. Also, secondary completion entails a "sheepskin effect" that signals ability and other relevant traits to potential employers, thereby enhancing access to better jobs—and a better life.

Although the prospective nature of this assumption on secondary completion and expected lifetime earnings precludes direct empirical support, evidence of a strong association between the secondary completion threshold and present income, especially for young adults and their families, lends it additional plausibility. Studies on three large and diverse countries in the region—Brazil, Peru and Argentina—find a very tight positive association between age-specific income and level of schooling (Brazil), and a comparably strong positive relationship between secondary completion by the household head and his/her household's per capita income (Peru and Argentina).[5]

The Basic Estimating Equation

The samples used for this study comprise poor and non-poor households. A logit regression is fitted where the dependent variable, secondary, is the simple dichotomy completing/not completing secondary education (1 and 0, respectively). The basic equation can be written as:

$$\text{Prob}(Secondary = 1) = F[c + \beta_1\, ED_{father} + \beta_2\, (D \times ED_{father}) + \beta_3\, ED_{mother}$$
$$+ \beta_4\, (D \times ED_{mother}) + \beta_5\, SIB + \beta_6\, (D \times SIB)$$
$$+ \beta_7\, GENDER + \beta_8\, (D \times GENDER) + \beta_9\, Y$$
$$+ \beta_{10}\, (D \times Y) + \beta_{11}\, MIGR + \beta_{12}\, (D \times MIGR)]$$

where F is a logistic function and the independent variables are all measured in 1985. These are: father's education (ED_{father}), mother's education (ED_{mother}), number of siblings (SIB), gender of the child with value one for male and zero otherwise ($GENDER$), household income (Y), and migration with value one if the child is a migrant and zero otherwise ($MIGR$). To distinguish poor from non-poor households, the regression also includes a corresponding set of variables formed by multiplying each of the indepen-

---

[5] See Aldaz-Carroll and Morán (2001).

dent variables by a dummy (*D*) with value one for household heads with primary education completed and zero otherwise.

Thus, the effect of any independent variable on the probability of secondary education completion of children from undereducated (assumed "poor") households can be distinguished from its effect on children from all other ("non-poor") households. Variables with a significant impact on the probability of secondary school completion of children born poor (i.e., the determinants of ITP) can thereby be identified.

Data

The "Lima Panel." The main limitation on social mobility research in Latin America has been the scarcity of panel data.[6] The only suitable panel data we found was constructed by Martin Cumpa from household surveys in Lima, Peru in 1985 and 1994 in connection with the Living Standards Measurement Study (LSMS). The panel consists of 856 individuals who, at the time of the second interview, were living in the same household in which they had been living at the time of the first interview. Our panel is a subset of individuals in Cumpa's panel with the required information for each independent variable. Information in the surveys goes back only nine years. Information from the 1985 survey is used as a proxy for circumstances pertaining to the individual's school years. For the 1985 data to be a good proxy of the schooling period, individuals in the 1994 survey should be chosen such that they are young enough to have been of school age in 1985, but old enough to have had ample opportunity to complete secondary education by 1994.[7] Thus, the age range for inclusion in our Lima panel sample is set at 16 to 26 years old in 1994, resulting in a panel of 294 individuals.[8]

The Latin American countries. To broaden the geographical scope of the investigation to other Latin American countries, we had to settle for a less accurate procedure. Looking only at individuals beyond secondary school

---

[6] Some initial trials have been done using simulated panel data. For example, the study for Colombia by Morley et al. (1998) leads to results that are sensitive to rather strong assumptions, including that mobility is only upward.

[7] In Peru, normal progression from first grade primary to secondary completion entails 11 years. Persons who received technical education and have at least 11 years of education are also considered to have completed secondary education.

[8] People over age 26 were also excluded because they are less likely to remain in the parental home and thus would not be captured in the 1994 survey, increasing sample attrition bias. Age 26 compromises between these considerations and sample size.

age in the sample, data on their educational attainment and that of their parents can be obtained from a single survey round. The value of the independent variables for that year is taken as a proxy of corresponding values during the person's school age. While these proxies are inferior to those in the Lima panel, key ones, such as parent's education, gender and, to a lesser extent, the number of siblings, are stock variables. This approach allows extending the study's scope to 15 additional Latin American countries that are home to most of the region's population, for which there is no panel data.[9] The sample consists of individuals between 20and 24 years old, on the assumption that anyone who has not completed secondary education by 24 is very unlikely to ever do so.[10] A cross-section logit regression is fitted for each country with dependent and independent variables defined analogously as for the Lima panel. A variable for residence was added, since most of the country surveys include both urban and rural areas.[11]

Results

Taking the unweighted average across the 16 Latin American countries with nationally representative data, 27 percent of children born poor complete secondary education compared to 63 percent of children born in non-poor households in the "typical Latin American country." By this count, intergenerational transmission of poverty traps about three of four children born in undereducated households in the typical country. As noted earlier, there were about 42 million such children at risk in Latin America in 1995. To ease exposition, we label the percent share of grown children[12] from the undereducated households who completed secondary school as the "poverty cycle break rate." Thus, the average rate in our sample of Latin American countries is 27 percent. We also use the term "probability of a child born poor (non-poor) completing secondary education" synonymously (analogously).

---

[9] The countries included are Argentina, Bolivia, Brazil, Chile, Colombia, Costa Rica, Ecuador, El Salvador, Honduras, Mexico, Nicaragua, Panama, Paraguay, Peru, Uruguay and Venezuela. The observations used are derived from the IDB Research Department's household survey data set.

[10] In the panel study the age range was extended to an interval of 16 to 26 years in a trade-off for a larger sample size.

[11] Data on migration was not available in the Latin America database.

[12] That is, those in the stipulated age group for ascertaining secondary school completion.

An ITP country ranking can be established based on this index (Figure 1). The probability that a child born poor will complete secondary education varies widely across the 16 countries, ranging from less than 10 percent in Honduras to 45 percent in Chile and above 50 percent in Bolivia and Peru.[13] Most of the countries, including the most populous, fall within the 10 to 30 percent interval.

ITP Factors: Descriptive and Analytical Results

Regression results for the Lima panel are shown in Table 1, while Table 2 shows the results for the 16 Latin American countries. In accordance with the basic estimating equation presented earlier, these tables show regression results for each primary independent variable (e.g., Father's education), as

---

[13] The values for Bolivia and Peru seem implausibly high. Despite our best efforts, we have been unable to identify a specific source of a possible overestimate. We suspect the presence of an artifact such as differences in survey coding procedures. Although not ideal, our statistical analysis is concerned with incremental differences in the index-related dependent variable *within each country*, which mitigates the consequences of *intercountry* differences in operational definitions.

FIGURE 1

Probability in Selected Latin American Countries that a Child Born Poor Will Complete Secondary Education

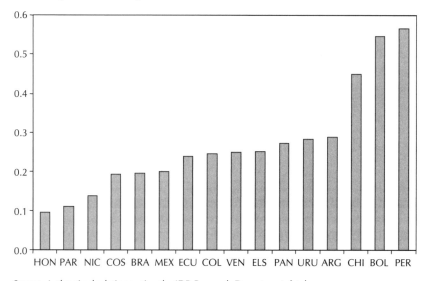

Source: Authors' calculations using the IDB Research Department database.

TABLE 1

Logit Estimates of the Probability of Completing at Least Secondary Education: Lima Panel Sample

Variable	Coefficient
Constant term	−1.233**
No. of siblings	−1.337**
No. of siblings * DR	1.329**
Father's education	0.879*
Father's education * DR	−0.894*
Mother's education	0.129
Mother's education * DR	−0.073
Gender	−0.539**
Household income	0.0004*
Household income * DR	−0.0004
Migration	2.350*
Migration * DR	−1.642
McFadden R^2	0.07
No. of observations	294

* Significant at 10% level.
** Significant at 5% level.

well as for the corresponding dummy variable, set as the product of its primary and a dummy value ("DR") equal to 1 for households headed by individuals with at least complete primary education and equal to zero otherwise. The coefficients for the primary variables pertain to undereducated ("poor") households and those for the dummy variables with "non-poor" households. Statistical technicalities aside, a practical way to regard the regression coefficients is in terms of their sign and statistical significance rather than their numerical values, which defy straightforward interpretation.

By and large, results are remarkably consistent in the sign and significance of the independent variables. For each variable, we briefly characterize its descriptive (i.e., zero order) association with corresponding rates of secondary completion and report its (*cet. par.*) statistical significance in the regressions. To assess and compare the magnitudes of the effect of significant ITP factors on the probability of secondary education completion, we also estimated the marginal or impact effects on a representative Latin American child born in a poor household of the corresponding variables based on regression results for the available countries. The representative

Cross-sectional Logit Estimates of the Probability of Completing at Least Secondary Education

(Dependent variable = 1 if at least secondary education completed; = 0 otherwise)

Variables	Brazil 1995	Chile 1994	Colombia 1995	Costa Rica 1995	Ecuador 1995	El Salvador 1995	Honduras 1996	Mexico 1994	Argentina¹ 1996	Bolivia¹ 1995	Uruguay¹ 1995
Constant	-2.966***	-1.613***	-1.828***	-3.178***	-1.935***	-2.595***	-2.999***	-2.121***	-2.253***	0.481**	-1.497***
No. of siblings	-0.227***	-0.180***	-0.111***	-0.084*	-0.191***	-0.142***	-0.295***	-0.229***	-0.244***	-0.167***	-0.353***
No. of siblings * DR	0.038	-0.297	-0.006	-0.195***	-0.036	0.286**	0.036	0.094**	—	0.096**	0.076
Mother's education	0.153***	0.145***	0.132***	0.070*	0.0221***	0.155***	0.107***	0.192***	0.232***	0.130***	0.108***
Mother's education * DR	0.002	0.013	0.057**	0.108**	-0.034	0.025	0.043	-0.038	—	—	0.021
Father's education	0.104***	0.060***	0.069**	0.152**	0.005	0.108***	0.040	-0.054	0.037	0.058***	0.124**
Father's education * DR	-0.041**	-0.001	0.012	0.069	0.066	-0.116***	0.078	0.110***	—	—	-0.068
Gender	0.038***	0.585***	0.513***	0.776***	0.369	0.488	0.522***	0.491***	1.137***	0.085	0.557***
Gender * DR	0.063	-0.040	0.040	—	0.270	-0.270	-0.233	-.329	0.416***	—	—
Household income	0.001***	0.000***	0.000**	0.000***	0.000	0.000***	0.000***	0.000***	—	—	0.000
Household income * DR	0.000***	0.000**	0.000**	0.000	0.000	0.000	0.000***	0.000	—	—	—
Residence	0.714***	0.777***	1.034***	1.212***	1.262***	1.132***	1.640***	0.912***	—	—	—
Residence * DR	0.445***	0.204*	-0.089	-0.545*	-0.443	-0.03	0.095	0.061	—	—	—
Single mother hhead	—	—	—	0.125	—	—	—	—	—	—	—
Single mother hhead * DR	—	—	—	1.665***	—	—	—	—	—	—	—
Mother works	—	—	—	0.269	—	—	—	—	—	—	—
Mother works * DR	—	—	—	-0.849***	—	—	—	—	—	—	—
Adoles. single mother	—	-0.754*	—	—	—	—	—	—	—	—	—
Adoles. single mother * DR	—	-0.154	—	—	—	—	—	—	—	—	—
Mc Fadden R²	0.27	0.22	0.21	0.27	0.26	0.27	0.34	0.27	0.25	0.12	0.15
No. of observations	15,209	9,355	5,446	1,466	1,127	1,984	1,397	3,209	580	1,310	3,267

*** Significant at the 1 percent level.   ** Significant at the 5 percent level.   *Significant at the 10 percent level.

¹ Urban survey.

Variable definition: *Residence* is a dummy that takes the value 1 if the person lives in an urban area and the value zero if the person lives in a rural area. The variable *single mother head of household* takes a value of 1 if the head of household is a single woman, and zero otherwise. The variable *mother works* takes a value of 1 if the mother is employed and zero otherwise.

child is statistically defined as a boy with three siblings, a mother with 2.8 years of education, and a father with two years of education, living in an urban area in a household with the average household income of undereducated households in the respective country.

Number of siblings. In general, the more siblings a poor child has, the lower his or her chances of completing secondary education. For the Latin American data, the negative relation is fairly mild for up to three siblings and quite strong for four or more. About 29 percent of the children with less than four siblings complete secondary schooling, compared with 18 percent of those with four or more siblings. In the full regressions, the coefficient for the siblings variable is significantly negative in the Lima panel and in each of the 16 Latin American regressions. In all regressions except for Lima and Costa Rica, the coefficient is significant at the 1 percent level. The more siblings a child born in poverty has, the less likely it is that the child will complete secondary education. The marginal effect of one more sibling on the probability of ITP averages 3.2 percentage points across the Latin American countries in the sample. For Panama, Ecuador and Mexico, this effect exceeds 4 points.

These results are predicted by the Beckerian model and are also consonant with most findings in the literature on determinants of schooling outcomes, such as those reported in Psacharopoulos and Arriagada (1989) for Brazil, Behrman and Wolfe (1987) for Nicaragua, and Birdsall (1980) for Colombia. In addition, a review of 18 country studies, including eight Latin American countries, concluded that children with fewer siblings are more likely to be wanted children, to access public resources, to be treated more equitably relative to their siblings, to receive more parental time, and to have lower fertility aspirations when they grow up (Lloyd, 1994). A large number of siblings in poor households almost inevitably has negative effects on child nutrition and hence on schooling.

Another notable result is that in five of the seven regressions in which the sibling effect is significantly different between poor and non-poor households, it is, as predicted by the Beckerian model, stronger in the poor households. The result was also expected because the pressure that the number of siblings puts on family resources is less severe in non-poor households. The income derived from parental work time is generally greater, and child rearing time more ample—that is, non-poor parents tend to work fewer hours and therefore have more time to spend with their children. Since these constraints on investing in children do not bite as hard, an additional child in

Secondary Education Completion by Father's Years of Education among 20-year olds Born Poor

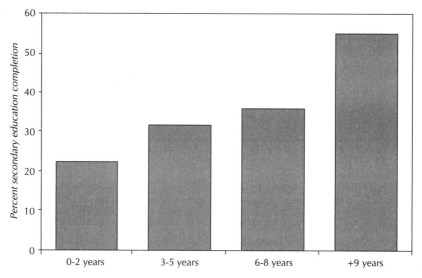

Source: Authors' calculations using the IDB Research Department database.
Note: Calculation based on an average of 16 Latin American countries with national data.

these household does not dilute the resources available per child as markedly, if it all, as it does in poor households.

Parental education. The father's education bears a marked positive association with our outcome (ITP) variable (Figure 2).[14] The marginal effect of more years of a father's education on the probability of ITP averages one percentage point for the 16 countries and is especially strong in Peru, Costa Rica and El Salvador.

The histogram depicting the probability of a poor child's secondary completion as a function of the mother's education is very similar to that for father's education, and the differences on ITP rates for the mother's education are even more marked. While the mother's education fails the significance test in the Lima panel regression—owing mainly to its colinearity with father's education—it has a positive and highly statistically significant

---

[14] Nine or more years of father's education in Figure 2 implies that the mother is the household head, has not completed primary schooling and thus the household (and hence the child) is classified poor.

effect in the country regressions.[15] The importance of a mother's education on children's schooling performance has been emphasized in the literature and documented in empirical studies (Schultz, 2001).

The marginal effect of one more year of mother's education on the probability of breaking the ITP cycle averages 2.3 points for the Latin American countries, more than twice the amount for father's education. For half the countries, the marginal effect is 3 points or higher.

In sum, the effect of parental years of schooling on the intergenerational transmission of poverty is generally significant, and the impact is appreciable. A common rationale in the theoretical models discussed previously is that more educated parents are more capable of assisting their children with their homework and usually have greater aspirations for their children, which motivates those children to achieve a higher level of education.

Gender. While 32 percent of girls born poor complete secondary education, only 22 percent of boys born poor do so. This substantial difference is strongly supported by the panel and the Latin American regressions, in which the gender coefficient was highly significant in women's favor, except for Bolivia and Ecuador, where it is not significant.[16] This result is consistent with other studies for Latin America (ECLAC, 1998).

The representative Latin American child's probability of completing secondary education increases on average by 11.5 percentage points if the child is a girl compared to the probability for a boy. For Argentina, Nicaragua, Costa Rica and Venezuela, the impact effect of gender is particularly strong.

The Beckerian model would explain this finding in terms of girls' lower opportunity costs of studying. This is supported by evidence that employment rates for girls who drop out of school in Latin America are much lower than for boys. Among 15 to 19-year olds living in urban areas in 11 Latin American countries, 16 percent of the women were gainfully

---

[15] The positive coefficient of a mother's education is insignificant for Nicaragua and in the Lima panel due to its substantial correlation with the father's education (i.e., assortative mating). When the father's education is dropped, the mother's education is significant, and its marginal effect becomes much larger. The education of the mother and that of the father are jointly significant in those regressions where either one is not significant. The marginal effects of the father's and mother's education in the Lima panel are sensitive to the inclusion of only one of the two variables or of both in the regression.

[16] Although in Bolivia and Ecuador the relevant coefficients show the probability of secondary education completion to be larger among women than among men, the difference was not statistically significant. In the other 14 Latin American countries the difference was highly statistically significant.

employed compared to 33 percent of men (ECLAC, 1998). These differences are even greater in rural areas.

Household income. Children's education is not an inferior good, and thus household income has a high statistically significant positive effect on the probability of overcoming ITP in the Lima panel and in all the Latin American regression results, except Ecuador.[17] Also, children in lower income households are often forced to drop out of school to supplement family income.[18]

In about half the Latin American regressions, the (positive) coefficient of household income on overcoming ITP is statistically significant and higher in poor households than in non-poor households. In the remaining countries, the coefficients are not significantly different. However, in terms of antipoverty policy strategy, a more interesting result is that even while significant, the marginal effect on the probability of ITP of a substantial (10 percent) increase in household incomes is typically small compared to parental education and other factors. On average, the marginal effect is less than 0.5 percentage points and in no cases does it reach 1 percentage point.

Migration. Because of limited data, the effect of migration on secondary completion could only be measured in the Lima panel regression. In the panel, migrant children are significantly less likely to complete secondary education than non-migrants, which suggests that the disruptions associated with migration during childhood, and lower school readiness by migrants, swamp the better education opportunities available in Lima. Other variables that could be included only in the country regressions are discussed below.

Urban/Rural residence. Poor children in Latin American urban areas complete secondary education at a rate that is well over twice that of their

---

[17] Household income in the Lima panel, as all other independent variables, is measured nine years back in time to capture household income during the person's school years. In the country regressions, income is measured for the year of the survey, and is our best proxy of household income during the child's school years.

[18] Direct and indirect (or opportunity) costs of education appear to be very important in the region, especially for secondary education. In Colombia, a 1992 study found that among households with children attending public school, households in the top quintile spent 1 percent of average income on primary education, while those in the bottom quintile spent 4.4 percent, in part because these families have more children. For children attending secondary school, families in the top quintile spent 1.7 percent of their income, compared to 10.9 percent of family income for the bottom quintile (IDB, 1998). Regarding opportunity costs, children aged 10 to 18 in rural Peru worked 37 hours per week if they were not enrolled in school and only 20 hours if they attended school (Gertler and Glewwe, 1989).

rural counterparts (34 vs. 13 percent). The regressions for the 13 countries where surveys covered both rural and urban areas showed residence to be a highly statistically significant variable. On average, the representative child's probability of completing secondary school falls by 14 percentage points if he or she lives in a rural area rather than in an urban area. In Peru and Ecuador, the negative impact exceeds 20 points.

The disadvantage of rural residence for secondary school completion is not confined to poor children. In most countries there is no statistically significant difference between the urban/rural impact on children born poor and non-poor.

López (1995) catalogues several possible reasons for low secondary completion rates in rural areas. Parents might value the opportunity cost of children as farm workers much higher than the present value of future returns to secondary education. Second, credit market imperfections in rural areas impede borrowing to cover the cost of keeping the child in school even if parents assess the economic returns to the child's secondary education to be sufficiently high. Third, as Becker (1975) argues, the cost of having a larger "quantity" of children is lower in rural areas, resulting in less "quality" investments per child. Fourth, accessibility and quality of secondary schooling are significantly lower in rural than in urban areas. Finally, returns to education are lower in rural than in urban areas because nonagricultural work requires more skills that correlate with higher levels of education than agricultural work (López and Valdés, 2000). Data and other limitations did not allow us to further analyze the reasons behind the urban/rural differential on ITP. A comprehensive analysis of the determinants of poverty in rural areas in Latin America is provided in López and Valdés (2000).

Single adolescent mothers. The variable single adolescent mother head of household is statistically significant only in the Chile regression. Since on a priori grounds and on the strength of other studies this factor can be presumed to be quite important to the intergenerational transmission of poverty in Latin America, we believe that the overly strong assumptions required in constructing the variable led to a poor index and hence to the results obtained. The statistical results discussed here refer therefore to the Chile regression. The children of adolescent single mothers complete secondary education in a much lower proportion than other children; and the impact effect on the representative child's probability of finishing secondary school is strongly negative (-13 points). This result coincides with findings by Buvinić et al. (1992) based on a sample of households in Santiago. A re-analysis of the sample used in that study, commissioned for the study presented here, indicates that adolescent motherhood's effect on the child's educational performance partly results from a higher incidence of malnutrition compared to other children, which in turn makes the former more likely to repeat school years.[19] Adolescent motherhood also contributes to ITP in ways not captured by our framework, notably through the additional obstacles it presents to the adolescent mother in completing secondary school, especially those arising from childcare responsibilities and discrimination at school. Moreover, there is evidence that adolescent motherhood is itself transmitted intergenerationally: teen mothers tend to beget teen mothers (Buvinić, 1997).

Early childhood care and development. A second Lima panel was constructed from the same Lima data set to measure the impact on school progress of having attended an early childcare program. Children who were three and four years old in 1985 were selected to determine whether they had completed primary school by 1994. The small size of the sample (57 children) prevented distinguishing according to poor vs. non-poor households, although household income is a variable in the regression.

For this sample, 85 percent of the children who had attended childcare programs had completed primary school by age 13, compared to 52 percent of those who had not attended. The effect of childcare attendance on primary completion is positive and statistically significant in a regression that controls for number of siblings, father's education, mother's education, and household income in 1985 (Table 3). From this regression, we estimated corresponding marginal-impact effects on the probability of a boy from a representative undereducated Lima household having completed primary school by age 13. The base case attributes for the household are such that the father and mother had completed 2 and 2.8 years of school, respectively; household income was $1.52 per capita per day; and the child had not attended childcare. The impact of childcare attendance turns out to be unexpectedly large.

In this regression, the coefficients of father's education and household income are statistically insignificant and, in any case, their impact is negli-

---

[19] In the Santiago data analysis, parental education and household income also significantly affect child stunting, which in turn affects school repetition.

> ### TABLE 3

**Lima Panel Subsample: Logit Estimates of the Probability of Completing
at Least Primary Education by Age 13**

(*Dependent variable: D = 1 if at least primary education completed by age 13;
= 0 otherwise*)

Variable	Coefficient
Constant	−4.764*
No. of siblings	0.610*
Father's education	0.051
Mother's education	0.316*
Household income[1]	−4.9E-05
Childcare program	2.107*
McFadden R[2]	0.21
No. of observations	57

Note: Dependent variable measured in 1994, independent variables measured in 1985.

[1] The variable *Childcare program* is a dummy variable with a value of 1 if child attended an early childcare program and zero otherwise.

* Significant at the 5 percent level.

gible (less than 1 percentage point for an additional year of father's education or for an increase of 10 percent in household income). An additional year of mother's education, however, increases the child's probability of primary completion by age 13 years by 3 points; having one additional sibling reduced the probability by 6 points. Having attended a childcare program increased the probability by 39 points. From prior studies on the effects of early childcare programs on school performance (such as Buvinić et al., 1992), we expected strong significance and impact results for this variable. It is likely, however, that our estimates exaggerate the magnitudes. Available knowledge supports the common sense notion that parents' degree of concern and activism for their children's mental development vary substantially, including within socioeconomic groups. Such differences will affect not only their decision (and efforts) to send the child to a preschool program, but also many other aspects of the child's home environment and nurturing. We suspect that our coefficients are capturing the effect of these unobservables, and hence resulting in much stronger estimates than would be the case otherwise.

As mentioned, a strong positive impact of development-oriented early childcare programs on educational attainment is also supported by previous empirical studies. Buvinić et al. (1992) found that two-thirds of poor children in Santiago, Chile had lower than expected educational performance owing to a lack of meaningful developmental care during their early years. There are several studies based on data from Chile, other Latin American countries, and elsewhere in the world that broadly support this finding (Deutsch, 1999). Notably, two empirical studies in the U.S. using randomized trials, research designs and follow-up interviews of children up to ages 15 and 27, respectively, provide exceptionally sturdy support to the view that quality early childcare and development services to poor children is one of the most effective tools for breaching ITP (Karoly et al., 1998; IDB, 1999).

Moreover, developmental early childcare not only helps the child's future but also allows mothers to continue their education, learn new skills, or work outside the home, thus improving the household economy and even increasing the rate at which they would otherwise succeed in overcoming their own ITP.

The signs, significance and values of the coefficients in the country regressions and in the main Lima panel are generally robust to moderate changes in specification. The McFadden R^2 of the cross-section logit regressions is highest for the Paraguay regression (0.42). This statistic is higher in the Peru countrywide cross-section regression than for the Lima panel, despite the more suitable data available for the latter. One reason is that the inclusion of the variable urban/rural residence in the countrywide sample has a high explanatory power, resulting in a considerable increase in the McFadden R^2.

In sum, the econometric results indicate that there are several family factors that significantly improve a poor child's chances of breaking out of the poverty trap: fewer siblings, more educated parents, more household income, urban residence, attending an early childcare program, and not having been born to an adolescent mother.[20]

Comparative Impact of Independent Variables

To assess which factors are most consequential with respect to the intergenerational transmission of poverty in Latin America, the strength of the cor-

---

[20] The adolescent motherhood result applies strictly only to the Chilean case and attendance in early childcare programs only to Lima.

responding effects of the independent variables were compared for judg-
mentally small changes in their value, i.e., "marginal" changes in the case of
scalar variables, and qualitative changes in the case of qualitative variables.
Such measures were made, in the first instance, for each of the countries in
the database, leading to comparisons of the strength of each variable *within*
each country and *across* the sample of countries.

A second assessment (Figure 3) compares the identically defined
"marginal" (for scalar variables) or "impact" (for qualitative variables)
effects of each independent variable in terms of its unweighted mean values,
each averaged over the 16 countries (except for residence, which is averaged
over 13 countries). The discussion in this section integrates several of the
findings already reported in connection with each significant ITP factor.

Holding all other factors constant at the stipulated levels, the effect of a
10 percent increase in household income on the probability that this representative Latin American child born in poverty will complete secondary
education is, on average, an increase of 0.5 percentage points. This surprisingly weak effect is also found in the Lima panel (0.4 percentage points),
where measurement of the income variable is less of a problem. The weak

FIGURE 3

**Marginal or Impact Effects on the Probability of Secondary School Completion
in the mid-1990s in Latin America**

(Mean values for 16 countries, in percentage points)[1]

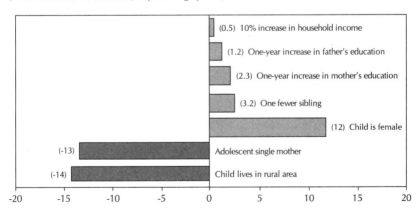

Source: Authors' calculations using the IDB Research Department database.

[1] Except for residence, which is based on 13 countries.

effect of income could owe partly to including parental education in the regression, which captures the permanent income effect, while the household income variable is mainly capturing the effect of transitory income on the probability of completing secondary. Excluding the education of the father and mother, the marginal effect of household income increases, but remains weak relative to the other factors.[21] While the magnitude of the marginal effect of household income is admittedly imprecise and always debatable, its relative weakness in our estimates is sufficiently marked and ubiquitous across countries to persuade us that ideal estimates would be unlikely to catapult household income into becoming the dominant factor. Moreover, this finding is supported by the Colombian study by López and Valdés (2000), in which the effect of one less sibling on the child's educational attainment was ten times larger than that of a 10 percent increase in per capita income.

Comparative results of the exercise on the impact of family factors on the probability of secondary school completion by the representative child can be summarized as follows. If the father had one more year of education, the child's probability of completing secondary school would increase by 1.2 percentage points. The corresponding effect of the mother's education is nearly double that of the father: 2.3 percentage points. If the child had one sibling less, probability of secondary school completion would increase by 3.2 percentage points. If the child were a girl rather than a boy, the probability would increase by 12 percentage points.[22] Having had an adolescent mother decreases probability by 13 percentage points. Living in a rural area decreases probability by 14 percentage points. In the Lima panel, had the child been a migrant, his or her probability of completing secondary school would drop by 24 percentage points.

Qualification of the Statistical Results

As with other statistical studies of this kind, the results reported here should be treated with caution. There could be problems of reverse causality, selec-

---

[21] Yet another worthwhile qualification is that an increase in household income sustained over the years is likely to have an indirect effect on ITP that is not captured in our estimated coefficient. For example, by inducing additional education or training of parents or older siblings, increased income would provide additional support for the child's schooling.

[22] The impact effect of gender in the Lima panel was 2 percentage points, which is lower than the regional average, but similar to the impact of gender in the Peruvian cross-sectional regression.

tivity bias, omitted variables, or measurement error, all of which could alter the estimated coefficient values and numerical results derived from them. However, the Lima panel results should be free of reverse causality, since the dependent variable lags the independent variables. Insofar as the results for the Latin American countries are consonant with those for the Lima panel, our concern for reverse causality seriously distorting the former is somewhat lessened. Owing to limitations in the available data, our statistical results are inevitably subject to the other problems mentioned.

Selectivity bias. In the Lima panel, individuals not reporting the same household head in both 1985 and 1994 surveys are excluded from the sample because they cannot be traced. In the Latin American country data, 20 to 24 year olds not living with their parents are excluded from the sample for lack of family background information. Those excluded from the samples probably had lower secondary school completion rates,[23] leading to biased estimates of the determinants of ITP. To overcome this limitation in this and most other studies on the subject would require an instrumental variable that affects the departure from the parental household but not educational achievement. We were unable to identify such a variable for this study. Devising one for subsequent work in this area is a worthwhile challenge.

The multiplicity of reasons why a 20 to 24 year old may not be living in the parental household further complicates the identification problem by requiring identification of multiple instrumental variables (Glewwe, 1995).

To the extent that selectivity bias in our estimates is deemed to be large, it can be regarded to apply properly only to the selected population of individuals still living in the parental household by ages 20 to 24. However, as argued by Glewwe (1995, p. 242), since the selection bias tends to make significant variables appear insignificant, "our estimates, by placing lower bounds on the effects of [the independent] variables, would still be useful for policy analysis."

In sum, the broad consonance of our results with the theoretical framework, with previous research, and among the Lima panel and country-specific regressions, provides a measure of confidence on the reliability of findings with respect to orders of magnitude and qualitative differentials.

---

[23] Among children born poor, those who could not be included in the Lima panel have a secondary completion rate of 27 percent, while for those included in the panel the rate is 34 percent.

The Effect of Other Factors on ITP

Data limitations prevented including in the regressions other likely family factors. This section discusses those other ITP factors using ancillary information.

Ethnicity. Although indigenous people make up only 10 percent of the Latin American population, they account for 25 percent of the region's poor and are more affected by intergenerational transmission of poverty than nonindigenous people (IDB, 1998). Whereas 36 percent of poor nonindigenous children had completed secondary education in Peru in 1994, only 23 percent of poor indigenous children had done so.[24]

Education tends not to be as good a proxy for indigenous people's socioeconomic well-being as it is for others. Years of schooling, together with other productive attributes such as age and experience, accounts for only half of their earnings gap relative to nonindigenous people. The remaining 50 percent earnings gap would reflect unaccounted factors such as discrimination, differences in infrastructure and access to services, quality of education, labor force participation, culture, or measurement errors.[25] A policy implication is that to effectively reduce the intergenerational transmission of poverty among indigenous people, household-oriented strategies to promote higher secondary school completion rates need to be complemented by measures to address socioeconomic issues such as those cited above. Nevertheless, family factors remain a crucial part of the strategy.[26]

Health. Children in undereducated households are more likely to be undernourished and to suffer from disease caused by poor sanitation and health practices, as well as from inadequate diets. This is usually compounded by environmental factors such as deficient health facilities. These health problems often hamper cognitive development among poor children, and all too often in cases of inadequate to severe malnutrition in early

---

[24] Authors' calculations using a survey database assembled by Instituto Cuánto (1994).

[25] According to Patrinos (1998), who argues that discrimination is the most important among such factors. However, a study of rural Peru by López and della Maggiora (1999) concludes that bias against indigenous villages in the supply of infrastructure and other public services is more important than discrimination.

[26] According to Chiswick (1988), "it would appear that members of more successful ethnic groups had parents with higher levels of schooling, fewer siblings to compete with for parental time and other family resources, and had mothers who were less likely to work when young children were in the household."

childhood, learning capacity is drastically impaired (Selowsky, 1978; Simmons and Alexander, 1980; Young, 1996). As mentioned earlier, child malnutrition was found to have a large impact on the probability of repeating a year of school in Santiago, Chile. In Guatemala, poor health was also linked to late school enrollment (Psacharopoulos, 1995, p. 7), and in rural Guatemala, nutrition was strongly related with school enrollment (Balderston et al., 1981).

Domestic violence. According to one estimate, some six million children in Latin America are severely abused at home (Larraín, 1997). While domestic violence is hardly unique to poor households, its effects are typically made worse by poverty (Morrison and Biehl, 1999). Domestic violence has a strongly negative impact on children's educational performance, even when the child is not the target. Moreover, children from violent homes tend to form violent homes as adults; in effect, an intergenerational transmission of violence.

A study by Morrison and Orlando (1997) in Chile found that children who experienced or witnessed domestic violence were significantly more likely to have disciplinary problems at school and to repeat grades. In that study's sample, 33 percent of children who suffered domestic violence had disciplinary problems at school, compared to only 13 percent of other children. The Chilean study by Larraín (1997) also showed that children who reported suffering abuse performed significantly worse in school than other students.

Non-family factors in ITP. As stated at the outset, this study deals only with a subset of factors that are known, or can be presumed to materially affect the intergenerational transmission of poverty. Some of the most obviously relevant among non-family or environmental factors that were left out of the study include accessibility to and the quality of basic social services available to the uneducated household. This includes reproductive and general health services, sanitation, and police protection (that is, services relating to the social environment), as well as labor market conditions for undereducated workers (affecting the "economic environment"). And although we have analyzed the role of household experience with certain social services, such as early childhood care and development programs, crucial aspects of accessibility and quality have not been addressed.

We are keenly aware of the advantages that incorporating such variables would have brought to the study, had it been feasible, and hope to see future research move in that direction. At the same time, we are reasonably confident that, despite the omission of these important components of the ITP picture, our main findings would not be qualitatively refuted by a more comprehensive analysis of the populations included in the samples. The main reason is our strong intuition that within each country sample (and especially for the Lima panel), the bulk of the households faced social and economic environments that were not sufficiently different across households to reverse our main results.[27]

Policy Implications

In terms of the overall economy, perhaps nothing is more important to most poor families than rapid and sustained economic growth that generates job opportunities, thereby raising income and moving future generations out of poverty. A stagnant economy offers little hope for breaking the poverty cycle. However, while robust economic growth may be indispensable, it may also bypass the poorest families whose workers lack the minimum skills to take advantage of job opportunities. Moreover, even when undereducated parents are able to find plenty of work in the wake of sustained economic growth, their children are likely to remain at serious risk of falling behind or failing at school, and consequently being unable to compete for jobs that could pull them out of poverty. These families also need more specific forms of support. Findings from our study provide strong guidance for devising strategies and programs to provide such support.

The findings in this study suggest that family factors play a major role in the educational attainment of poor children in the region and, hence, on their lifetime economic prospects. The regression results show that children who are far more likely to complete secondary education and break the ITP cycle are those with fewer siblings, one parent with at least a few years of primary schooling, relatively higher household income, and who reside in urban areas and, in particular, have attended preschool. While these results are not unexpected, and broadly reinforce earlier findings, they are notable for the consistency of the effects of the variables across countries and of the

---

[27] Even if the omitted variables affected poor households very differently, the results would not be biased significantly if the omitted variables were not strongly correlated with the independent variables.

generally large impact of the mother's education, even at low levels, on her children's secondary education. Most notable is the extraordinarily strong effect of preschool attendance in the Lima panel.

Most family factors affect the demand side of educational investments and of other child quality indicators that help break the ITP cycle. Most poverty-oriented public policies and programs, however, focus on supply-side factors such as extending the coverage of public schools and health facilities to the poor. Although critically important for poor families, the traditional supply-side strategy may not be sufficient to overcome family constraints. In particular, public education, especially if its quality is poor, may be insufficient to shift parental preferences towards lower fertility (less quantity) and more schooling of each child (more quality).

Thus, while unambiguously supporting the common recommendation to improve the quality of health and education services available to children of the poor, the study's main policy implication is the crucial need to complement such supply-side actions with coherent interventions focused on under-educated families, all within an integrated plan to break the poverty cycle. The remainder of this section sets out the key ingredients of such a plan.

Comprehensive Support to Families

Government policies that combat poverty have largely overlooked the role of parents in the transmission of poverty or wealth to their children, and have not taken advantage of the impetus that parents can provide to their children. The tendency has been to concentrate on either parents or children as independent recipients of services, as if they existed independently from their families and, for that matter, from their economic and social environment. Yet, with appropriate support, poor parents can become a powerful force in building their children's human capital, thereby improving their prospects for the future. Poverty among future generations can be reduced faster and more efficiently if parents receive adequate support.

In the context of the household unit, there are several ways to provide parents, children and entire families with complementary services that improve both their present well-being and their children's prospects of escaping the poverty cycle. The most promising services in the Latin American context entail quality public interventions in the areas of reproductive health, education and training for adolescents and young adults (especially mothers), prevention of domestic violence, reductions in the disadvantage of rural residence, and, most importantly, early childcare and development. When the target families are from indigenous cultures, such interventions must be adjusted accordingly.

Reproductive Health Services and Education

This study confirms that the links between high fertility (in terms of number of siblings) and the intergenerational transmission of poverty are quite strong, suggesting useful interventions for helping break the poverty cycle. Particularly powerful options are to provide high-quality family planning and other reproductive health services to all women and men, including adolescents. By reducing the number of unwanted births, these programs heighten parental appreciation for their existing children as well as their propensity to invest in them. Since fewer children in a poor household implies more resources available per child, these two effects of reproductive health services mutually reinforce one another in boosting parental investments in their children. The programs also provide incentives to postpone the start of childbearing. The effectiveness of these services can be enhanced by concurrent measures to reduce discrimination against women.

Yet, parental education must go beyond traditional family planning to include larger issues of parental responsibilities and effective child-rearing practices, children's rights, and, when parents are separated or divorced, adequate social and economic protection for women and children. Parenting education can be integrated into the high school curriculum and be supplemented and extended to the population as a whole through mass media campaigns.

Education and Training for Young Parents, Especially Mothers

The results of this study show that the mother's education—even as a little as an additional year of primary school—plays a critical role in increasing the probability that her children will complete secondary education. This is true in all the countries studied. Thus, supplementary adult education, including well designed literacy programs, and especially those geared to young mothers, have significant payoffs for current and subsequent generations—in effect, it is an investment with an unending stream of future benefits.

Skill Training for Young Adults

As noted earlier, the combination of low quality and insufficient schooling for impoverished youth constrains their access to better jobs and hence the path out of poverty. However, there are some countries that have vigorous institutions and effective programs that provide young people the opportunities to gain skills as an adult and move to a job with at least the potential of leading to above-poverty income. Such programs include high quality, low cost, and convenient courses in vocational and technical schools geared to those already working; well established craft apprenticeship programs, such as those in Germany; and realistic government incentives for firms to provide on-the-job training to workers. Unfortunately, there are too few such programs in Latin America, and those that do exist, such as the SENAI/SENAC programs in Brazil and *Chile Joven* in Chile, tend to cover only a small portion of lower-skilled people from disadvantaged families.

Supporting Indigenous People[28]

The prevalence of malnutrition among indigenous people is twice that of the rest of the population, and far worse than expected after adjusting for key socioeconomic factors, including rural residence. Along with information on poverty, social infrastructure, child development, and disease, these statistics also depict the depth of disadvantage among indigenous peoples (Psacharopoulos and Patrinos, 1994). Malnutrition not only diminishes the present well-being of its victims, but also perhaps even more tragically stunts the mental development of affected children and impairs the lifetime prospects of future generations. Immediate remedies are needed.

Short-term efforts to improve nutrition, especially among young indigenous children, must reinforce the positive elements of community knowledge and practices and try to change or improve the negative ones. Where necessary, family-targeted programs should include the provision of subsidized nutrients and incentives for their appropriate intake. The longer-term strategy must provide the necessary social infrastructure, including culturally appropriate and good quality health care, safe water and sanitation;

---

[28] This section draws heavily on McGuire (1998).

child development programs, pre-schools and primary education; and social safety nets.

Most indigenous development specialists hold that to increase their effectiveness, programs aimed at breaking the poverty cycle need to be tailored to the cultural characteristics of the communities and should involve them, and the families themselves, in designing and running the programs. There is growing political consensus in Latin America that extra efforts should be made to help indigenous communities, despite the expectedly higher cost of such tailor-made programs. Countries with large indigenous populations must effectively extend coverage of all basic public services to them if they are to overcome persistent poverty in the foreseeable future.

Some specialists also recommend disaggregating social indicators and service statistics by ethnic group to identify particular problems and track progress. In Mexico, for example, the poverty map used for targeting the coverage of *Oportunidades* and other poverty reduction programs includes the proportion of indigenous people as a critical dimension. The data show that most highly marginal communities are predominantly small indigenous communities.

Preventing Domestic Violence

While domestic violence is not restricted to poor families, it does compound poverty-related problems. Domestic violence demands appropriate legislation and police and judicial systems attuned to the issue; it also requires abatement actions such as counseling habitual aggressors and victims. Although legislation in most countries in the region is adequate, implementation is weak. Judges and the police need to be trained to become more sensitive to the problem and effectively apply existing laws. Emergency telephone lines with direct links to specialized police personnel and community assistance centers can reduce the incidence and consequences of domestic violence, notably including its lasting emotional and behavioral effects on children.

The health system should also play a key role. Detection of domestic violence by health care workers and referrals to specialized services, or appropriate authorities, are key ingredients in strategies to reduce domestic violence that are often absent in the countries of Latin America. Counseling and follow-up measures to assist families prone to domestic violence should be systematically included among the health system's responsibilities.

Ultimately, prevention of violence is the most effective way of dealing with the problem, and education is the most effective route to prevention. Increasing personal awareness of the issue through early detection workshops for parents, teachers and children can go a long way toward preventing and reducing domestic violence and mitigating its effects on children. Conflict resolution techniques and other approaches, which have been shown to be effective in preventing violence, can also be introduced into school curriculum. In addition, mass media campaigns are an effective tool to raise awareness about domestic violence and make information about assistance programs for victims and their children widely available.

Reducing the Disadvantage of Rural Residence

Poor rural areas in the region typically lack not only adequate social services, but also suitable infrastructure and services to support economic production, including technical assistance and credit and marketing services. Lack of access to quality education, combined with the substantial productivity of children in agricultural work, is a formidable combination of forces hobbling the educational attainment of rural children, especially boys. Rural children in all 16 countries in this study have significantly lower probabilities of completing secondary school than urban children.

Programs to tackle the ITP cycle in rural areas should particularly address demand factors in conjunction with supply-side actions affecting investment in children. Policies to increase the physical assets of poor families include land titling and distribution programs, and improving access to credit markets and modern inputs. These and other strategies to address rural poverty in the region are persuasively set out in López and Valdés (1998).

Programs for Young Children

As shown by the statistical results for the Lima panel, children from undereducated households who participated in preschool programs were far more likely to complete secondary school. Early childcare and development programs have been found to provide many benefits to parents, children and society at large.[29] For example, these programs allow parents, especially mothers, to increase their labor force participation and earnings, increase their work experience, and work more hours. Children benefit from improved health care and nutrition, early stimulation, and other developmental activities provided by most of these programs. They also benefit later in life from higher educational attainment and greater earnings. Older primary and secondary school-aged children also benefit because they will not be called upon to care for their younger brothers or sisters at the expense of schoolwork. They and their parents will also have more resources available to them as a result of increased public spending on the younger siblings (see Castañeda, 1979). The benefits to society include lower incidence of antisocial behavior and juvenile delinquency, as documented in randomized longitudinal studies for certain early childhood care and development programs in the United States (see Karoly et al., 1998).

Despite the powerful and cost-effective results of early childhood intervention programs, especially in breaking the intergenerational transmission of poverty, coverage remains very low in Latin America. It is estimated that less than 20 percent of poor urban children under six years of age participate in childcare and development programs. Coverage is even lower in rural areas and for indigenous populations, for whom in most countries childcare models have yet to be adequately developed or tested. Governments, civil society organizations and the private sector should assign the highest priority in the battle against ITP to rapidly increase coverage of quality early childcare and development services among the poor.

Programs for Primary and Secondary Students

Educating a child is generally expensive. For the poor families in Latin America, it is prohibitively expensive. Because education entails substantial costs over many years, poor people find it very difficult to finance investments in education, despite their high rates of return. Moreover, unlike other long duration investments such as a home, human capital cannot be put up as collateral for investment loans.[30] Yet, government support for

---

[29] Deutsch (1998) reviews these programs and Morán and Myers (1999) provide a policy-oriented treatment of the issues.

[30] Even in cases where investments can be put up as collateral, cash flow problems can be a great obstacle to profitable long-term investments by the poor, as has been shown in reforestation

investments in education by the poor is mostly limited to tuition waivers. Sometimes food is also included, especially in public preschools, although they cover only a small proportion of the children in poverty. Living expenses, especially food and shelter, in addition to outlays for uniforms, school supplies, and transport, which may account for a significant part of the costs, must be borne by parents, other family members or the students through part-time work. These direct costs have most likely increased in recent years as a result of urbanization, especially in the face of the urban segregation of low-income communities. In addition to the direct costs of paying for education, indirect costs in terms of the income foregone while attending school must also be borne by the families. Particularly at the secondary level and beyond, these costs tend to loom even larger.

There are several ways that government programs can help the poor overcome the budget constraints that often impede educational invest-ments. The first is to provide scholarships that finance not only tuition costs but also maintenance and transportation costs for students from poor households. In Honduras, for instance, the *Bono Escolar* program has increased enrollment and reduced dropout rates significantly by giving mothers about $4 per month per child attending primary schools in selected poor areas (Castañeda, 1998). Families have used the additional resources largely for basic food and school supplies for the children.

A second instrument is to directly provide school-related items, such as uniforms, books and school meals for the poorest students. With a few notable exceptions (Chile and Costa Rica), formal school lunch programs are rare in Latin America.[31] School breakfast programs are rarer still, though their effect on school performance may be greater than school lunches. A study that estimated that up to two-thirds of children go hungry at least some of the time in U.S. inner cities, also found that poor children who were given free breakfast in school did better, felt happier and found it eas-

---

projects in many countries in the region. Under traditional, collateralized, financial arrangements, poor families do not have the savings to cofinance the recurrent costs needed to support such projects to maturity and support their families during the long investment periods.

[31] In many countries there are a number of formal or informal programs that provide some form of nourishment to schoolchildren. These include "glass of milk" programs, enriched cookies, or school lunches prepared at school with donated foods from international sources. In many cases, these programs provide only a small portion of the calories and proteins required by the students, and the food supplements are often unavailable because of budget shortages, mismanagement or corruption, or inadequate food supplies.

ier to learn (see *The Economist*, September 19-25, 1998). It is safe to say that the proportion of poor children who are hungry in Latin America is higher.

A third mechanism involves quality reproductive health, family planning and "life-style" education programs for adolescents. Reducing adolescent pregnancy, drug abuse and violence will go a long way toward reducing the transmission of poverty across generations. As noted previously, teen pregnancy is known to result in the end of schooling for the teen mother and in the birth of children who suffer from ill health and deprivations that affect learning and impede their way out of poverty (Buvinić, 1998; Maynard, 1996).

Efforts are underway in many countries to improve the quality of education through better teacher training, improved facilities and materials, and new technologies. While these efforts are commendable and should result in better public schools and reduce the private-public quality gap, to increase school retention or reduce the dropout rates of poor children substantially they must be accompanied by measures to increase effective demand for education among the poor through income support and other programs such as those profiled here.

Integrating Programs around the Family

Integrating programs around the family is essential to take advantage of complementarities among programs and to support parents in investing in their children. Yet, in practice, integrating programs is difficult because each one is the responsibility of a different agency and because the "family," as such, has not been a focus of social policy. However, three innovative examples of coordinated social programs currently in implementation are worth noting: *Oportunidades* in Mexico (formerly known as *Progresa*), the Family Allowance Program (PRAF) in Honduras, and *Bolsa Escola* in Brazil.

Oportunidades in Mexico

Mexico launched the *Oportunidades* program in mid-1997 to combat poverty through integrated family interventions in education, health and nutrition. *Oportunidades* is a massive program. By the end of 1999, it covered approximately 2.6 million families or about 40 percent of all rural families and more than 10 percent of all Mexican families. At the time,

Oportunidades operated in almost 50,000 localities in 31 states. Yet, its budget of about $777 million in 1999 corresponded to less than one-quarter of 1 percent of Mexico's GDP.

In education, *Oportunidades* provides cash payments to mothers whose children regularly attend school from the third grade to the third year of secondary school (a schooling level found to have high levels of attrition). Allocations for girls who remain in school receive a premium. The value of the education grants to parents takes into account the estimated economic contribution to the family by children who drop out of school (Skoufias and McClafferty, 2001). The program operates only in localities with a primary school and relatively good access to a secondary school of acceptable quality.

The health component includes a basic health care package containing mother/child, prenatal, and well-baby care, and food supplements for pregnant mothers and malnourished or at-risk children. Families enrolled in the program also receive nutrition and hygiene education. Food supplements to meet about 20 percent of caloric needs and up to 100 percent of micronutrient needs are also provided to undernourished mothers and children at the health clinics.

As part of the health and nutrition component, *Oportunidades* also provides cash "food support" to the mothers of participating families. Nutrition education and community participation activities ensure that the additional income improves the food intake and nutrition of family members, especially children and pregnant and lactating mothers. The monthly cash transfers are contingent on all family members visiting health centers for required checkups and nutrition and hygiene education, and on school-age children attending school regularly.

Oportunidades works in conjunction with programs promoting employment and income opportunities. It also includes coordinated efforts to enhance the ability of educational and health services to meet increased demand resulting from implementation of the program itself.

Direct cash assistance supplements family income and can be spent on any food item or other necessity. For an average poor family, the cash supplement was 235 Mexican pesos in 1997, or about 34 percent of recipient income. On the assumption that women are more concerned about the nutritional needs of the family and children, all financial assistance (scholarships and cash for food) is given to the mother every two months.

A recent evaluation of the program, based on a powerful semi-experimental research design, reports that over the two-year period from November 1997 to November 1999, *Oportunidades* showed significant success in meeting its main objectives (Skoufias and McClafferty, 2001). For example, as a result of program activities (i.e., compared to the control group), school enrollment increased (especially of girls and at the secondary school level), implying that children in the locations covered by *Oportunidades* will average at least 0.7 more years of schooling. This gain is expected to increase as proportionately more of the children progress toward secondary school completion. As a result of the higher schooling, the children's expected lifetime earnings are estimated to be 8 percent greater. Children in the program have a 12 percent lower incidence of illness and adults experience 19 percent fewer disability days. The impact of *Oportunidades* on nutrition is also noteworthy. It has significantly reduced the probability of physical stunting among one to three-year old children. Channeling all monetary benefits to women has increased their say in their household decisions.

While it is too soon to tell the extent to which *Oportunidades* will reduce ITP in rural Mexico, its design and implementation to date, along with the results of the intermediate evaluation, generally support a measure of optimism. *Oportunidades* is an excellent model for countrywide programs to tackle the intergenerational transmission of poverty in Latin America, although the results of several studies on the determinants of ITP suggest that the program has one major problem. To date, *Oportunidades* lacks a component to tackle the critical deficiencies in early childcare and development that affect the vast majority of children in the population group encompassed by the program. In particular, *Oportunidades* notably and regrettably lacks interventions to improve psychomotor and cognitive development.

The Family Allowance Program (PRAF) in Honduras

The Family Allowance Program (PRAF) began in 1990 as a social safety net to mitigate the impact of macroeconomic adjustment on the poor. The program was restructured in 1998, and now includes a reformulated project known as PRAF/IDB, Phase II. Its central objective is to encourage poor households to invest in their family's education and health by providing incentives to increase the use of preventive health services, increase primary school attendance, and improve the quality of educational and health care services. The program also includes a monitoring and evaluation component to promote accountability and to assess program impact over time.

PRAF's key features include two incentive programs to stimulate demand for human development services and interventions that enhance the supply of such services. One program is focused on poor children attending primary school (*Bono Escolar*). In this program, vouchers (*bonos*) are distributed to mothers at schools in certain localities, conditioned on the child's regular school attendance. Beneficiaries can use the vouchers to purchase food, school supplies and medicines. According to early studies, most recipients spent over 80 percent of the voucher value on food. The other program is targeted to children up to 5 years old and to pregnant and nursing mothers (*Bono Materno Infantil*). Under this program, food is distributed at health posts and centers in selected poor localities to eligible mothers and children, conditioned on visits for regular health check-ups and vaccinations.

Brazil's Bolsa Escola

Initiated by the government of the Federal District of Brasilia in 1995, this project provides income support for very poor families with children 7 to 14 years of age attending public schools. By mid-1997, over 44,000 children from 22,000 families had received benefits under the program. The annual cost was $19 million, or less than 1 percent of Brasilia's government budget.[32] Another program (*Poupanca-Escola*) seeks to reduce repetition and dropout rates by providing a financial incentive to parents and children to complete secondary education. The government provides a stipend to the family on the condition that the student passes his or her grade (see IDB, 1998). Both programs are showing promising results: repetition and dropout rates have decreased for those participating in the program.

Other Programs

Some countries are also experimenting with vouchers to improve the income of poor farmers in order to encourage them to invest in their

[32] See idrc.ca/lacro/foro.

children's health and education. In Colombia, a pilot voucher program will soon be introduced in poor marginal areas. The program will benefit farmers with less than five hectares of land whose average family income per month is below the extreme poverty line. Program participation requires that all school-age children in the farmer's household attend school regularly, that their young children fulfill a required vaccination schedule, and that the family participates in the government's program of basic health services. The basic package includes mother/child preventive and curative interventions, reproductive health and nutrition education, and outpatient services for all family members. A monitoring and evaluation system will ensure that eligibility conditions for all beneficiaries are maintained during the duration of the project.

Implementing Integrated Family-focused Programs

The implementation of integrated family-focused programs is difficult. Ensuring coordination between the various agencies that need to be involved (e.g., education, health and nutrition, statistical and agricultural agencies, NGOs) is complicated and time consuming. The agency created to administer the program in Honduras (PRAF) faced several problems, beginning with weak administrative capacity for managing critical tasks such as registering beneficiaries, printing, distributing and redeeming stamps, and carrying out budgeting and accounting activities. Other problems included unresponsiveness by health centers and posts to requests by potential beneficiaries to register in the program, and inadequate program monitoring and evaluation.

It is critically important that the agencies involved have the political and economic incentives to participate actively and with a sense of ownership (or, at least, accountability) in fulfilling their assigned functions. Also crucial is that controls be in place to ensure that the services provided are of adequate quality. Public education, especially in rural areas, typically fails to meet any reasonable standard of quality. There is no point in requiring parents to send their children to school if teachers are often absent or the instruction imparted is of no value to the children's educational development, and hence, of no value to their parents. Health services, in particular, must be provided on a timely basis and meet quality standards. Poor parents, especially mothers who are usually the ones responsible for taking children to health service facilities, cannot afford the expense and the time often needed to travel long distances to health posts, only to then have to wait endlessly to consult with a health service worker who is oftentimes neither suitably qualified nor motivated.

Another important matter in designing family-focused anti-poverty programs is that of unintended perverse incentives. A major issue here is how to help poor families and their children without creating dependency and destroying the motivation for self-help and self-reliance. A related and particularly vexing problem arises when targeting malnourished children. These programs may often have the unintended effect of rewarding inappropriate or negligent nutritional practices by parents. In other cases, programs may end up being seen as entitlements to be available on a permanent basis as long as eligibility criteria continue to be met. Income-based eligibility criteria can discourage beneficiaries from earning more if the additional income makes them ineligible, thereby jeopardizing their program benefits. An example is the social security reform in Colombia that created a subsidized health insurance package for the poorest. Once someone is selected for a program, political forces often make it difficult to "graduate" a family or individual even if they rise above poverty (Castañeda, 1997).

Ways to deal with these unintended consequences include clearly stipulating entry and exit mechanisms at the outset, including maximum time limits for some or all benefits. Establishing a time schedule by which program benefits are reduced automatically is generally preferable to removing all benefits at once, which often generates strong political pressure opposing termination.

Targeting Family-focused Programs

The earlier discussion made clear that the integrated and family-focused programs recommended as a basic strategy to break ITP in Latin America are neither cheap nor easy to implement. Despite these drawbacks, the model is justified, essentially because it can be expected to work far better than current practices in the region, which evidence shows are functioning unacceptably in most countries.

One reason for the prevailing problems stands out, which is the failure to provide the comprehensive array of services needed to break the cycle of

ITP. There are strong complementarities among several of the major factors that can pave the way out of ITP, and hence among the services that would address them. For example, an expectant mother's prenatal care, good health and nutrition are generally essential for the child to be born without significant physical or mental impairment, which in turn is highly complementary with the child's early development, schooling achievement, and so on. Thus, in the abundant cases of babies conceived in extreme poverty in the region, where families lack the wherewithal to independently provide or buy adequate prenatal, maternal-child or early child health care, it is not enough for the public sector to deliver one or even several (but not all) of the services needed to break the ITP cycle. Nor is it enough if all services are available but the families do not demand them in a timely way, or if the available services are of insufficient quality.

Social expenditures meant to address the needs of poor families in most Latin American countries today typically are spread over a large number of programs and beneficiaries, without much attention to the complementarities entailed in the intergenerational transmission of poverty. The provision of all the necessary ingredients for destitute families to succeed in breaking ITP is rare. The relatively substantial social expenditures for services for extremely poor people are consequently not having a commensurate impact on reducing ITP, even among the assiduous clients of the services.

A service package sufficiently comprehensive to ensure a high success rate in breaking the ITP cycle among the poorest families in the region— including training to improve parental income, integrated child development programs, full-fledged scholarships in primary and secondary education, school breakfasts and lunches, adolescent programs, etc.— would cost significantly more than what governments are presently spending on conventional poverty programs. Thus, it would be politically unfeasible and economically prohibitive in most cases to make such a package available to all takers, especially with the same level of subsidy required for the poorest. With few if any exceptions, integrated ITP-oriented programs could only be put in place in Latin American countries if they were targeted and restricted to those households that are mired in the poverty trap.

Today, advances in information gathering and processing technology make effective targeting and monitoring possible in Latin America. Chile's *Ficha CAS* system pioneered efforts for the massive application of targeting criteria by local governments. Similar systems are now in place in a number of countries, including Colombia, Costa Rica and Mexico (particularly for the *Oportunidades* program). Colombian families that receive a variety of benefits, including health insurance, are selected through a two-stage means testing process. In the first stage, the poorest localities or neighborhoods within cities are selected on the basis of census information on basic sanitary services, schools, health facilities, dispersed populations and other socioeconomic indicators. In the second stage, the poorest families in those poorest localities are selected on the basis of family information regarding the quality of housing, public services, literacy, occupation, disability of family members and income.[33] Household targeting within "second stage" disadvantaged neighborhoods is controversial. Critics argue that such targeting harms the community's social fabric by dividing its members, most of whom are poor, between those who are deemed program beneficiaries and those who are left out.

In the same vein, it is possible to introduce features into most programs that make them more attractive to those families that would have been selected in a second-stage targeting exercise. For example, mother-child care and development centers, or any other service delivery site related to the program, can be studiously located in sectors of the neighborhood where the poorest families tend to agglomerate. Together with cosmetic features also designed to be less attractive to the more affluent members of the community, and targeted marketing within the neighborhood, a substantial degree of self-targeting can be achieved with little of the costs associated with administratively stipulated household targeting.

Aside from political and judgmental assessments of the drawbacks of second-stage household targeting, the choice of targeting system should take into account the features of the program and the communities that would be covered. Regarding the latter, the more uniformly poor the communities or the more spatially clustered the households according to the relevant ideal selection criteria, the less the economic benefits derived from administrative targeting.

Targeted social programs can also be effectively combined with urban rehabilitation, disaster prevention measures in vulnerable areas, and the

---

[33] See Gomez de Leon (1998) and Velez, Castaño and Deutsch (1998).

relocation or resettlement of families in ways that capitalize on complementarities between the interventions. For example, the usefulness of community centers, schools and health clinics provided through urban rehabilitation projects can be enhanced if the requirements of a concurrent targeted social program are taken into account when the facilities are designed and sited.

Conclusions

As in most places in the world over the course of history, in Latin America there is a strong link between the socioeconomic status of parents and their grown children. In all 16 countries analyzed for this book, parental education and family income were strong determinants of the probability that a child would complete secondary education (the minimum level considered necessary for permanently escaping poverty). Moreover, the family's demographic structure, particularly the number of siblings that a child has, is a powerful determinant, as is rural or urban residence. An important result is that the effects are quite consistent among countries and occur even at low levels of parental education. The implication is that while the problem is great, there are also levers connected to the family unit for breaking the intergenerational transmission of poverty.

The strong positive impact of parental schooling points to the large payoff from enhancing education for young parents and adults, as well as those likely to be involved in child-rearing. The strong negative impact of the number of siblings on the chances of completing secondary education is consistent with the quantity-quality theory of fertility and education of children, which emphasizes the roles played by parental constraints of time and resources in raising a family. The more children parents have, the more difficult it is for them to invest sufficiently in each child's health, education and other components of human capital. This is even more so for single mothers.

Although not included in this study's statistical analysis for lack of suitable data, the link between the socioeconomic status of parents and their children is also substantial in indigenous populations, as shown by our review of previous studies. Indigenous children have markedly lower levels of education and secondary school completion than nonindigenous children. In addition to the family factors found to be significant for the under-educated households at large, discrimination in educational opportunities and in the labor market reduces the economic value of education for this group. Indigenous populations are also twice as likely to suffer from malnutrition than nonindigenous people owing to inferior food security, diets, health services and nutritional education, among other factors. Policies to reach indigenous populations need to address these shortfalls through culturally appropriate versions of family-focused ITP programs. At the same time, incentive systems should be put in place to reinforce laws to combat discrimination.

As is usual in studies such as this one, the variables for which adequate information was available for inclusion in the basic statistical model inevitably leave a sizeable amount of "unexplained variance" in the probability that a child will complete secondary education. Additional regressions, tailored to more limited data found for other relevant factors, were also performed. Variables found to be statistically significant in these subsidiary regressions included early childhood education in Peru and teen pregnancy in Chile, both of which resulted in very strong positive and negative effects, respectively. Moreover, a mother's health and nutrition, and domestic violence, have also been shown in research reviewed for this study to have material consequences on children's educational prospects. While domestic violence and teen pregnancy are not confined to poor families, their occurrence tends to interact with other unfavorable, poverty-related factors to result in even worse consequences on the well-being and future prospects of children.

Our findings on the effects of family background variables on investments in children imply that demand-side factors play a crucial role in determining education outcomes. Most public policy, however, has focused on supply-side factors, notably the provision of schools and, increasingly, school materials, teacher training and other elements associated with the quality of the education. Regarding the supply of schools, the almost universal enrollment of children at the beginning of the school year, together with high repetition and dropout rates, tell us that lack of school places as such is no longer a critical impediment to educational progress and the reduction of endemic poverty in most Latin American countries. Concerning the quality of education still being offered to most children from poor families, however, all indications are that it remains dismally low and that much more needs to be done to improve it.

Public Policies to Break the ITP Cycle

To be effective, the design and implementation of programs to break the ITP cycle should take into account three basic propositions.

First, the family plays a crucial role in determining whether children succeed or fail in school, and hence on their prospects for breaking out of the poverty cycle. The effects of family factors can range from strongly positive to strongly negative and tend to be synergistic and interdependent.

Second, programs must maximize beneficial spillover effects of programs on family interactions. For instance, integrated early childhood programs provide benefits to parents as well as children. Parents, especially mothers, can increase their participation in the labor market and earn higher wages. Parents can also reduce their spending on food inasmuch as children who participate in some public programs may be given free breakfasts or lunches. This frees up resources to better feed other children or themselves. Older children also benefit because they will no longer be called upon to care for their younger brothers and sisters at the expense of attending school. All children and adults in the household will benefit from parenting instruction and support services provided by better childcare and development programs. The family will also benefit from timely referrals to other family support services, such as those for the prevention of domestic violence and for reproductive health.

Third, to understand family constraints and the process by which poverty—or its obverse, capital—are transmitted, it is important to consider the family life cycle, particularly elements of formation and reproduction, as well as parental labor force participation and earnings cycles. Especially among undereducated Latin Americans, childbearing begins at a time when parents are in the best position to take advantage of formal education and other skill improvement opportunities and to increase earnings from heightened opportunities for occupational mobility and migration. Early childhood care and development programs allow parents to capitalize on such opportunities to enhance their own human capital and earnings. Even though public school is typically tuition-free in the region, supporting children in school, especially in secondary school, requires relatively large outlays by parents, especially among the poor. These expenditures must be sustained over long periods when undereducated parents face stagnant earnings and little upward mobility. Integrated education programs for these children, which may include full scholarships (tuition and maintenance), school breakfast and lunch programs, and textbooks and materials, would go far in making it feasible for poor families to keep their children in school through the secondary cycle.

Some Latin American countries have designed integrated programs with a family focus. Two notable examples are *Oportunidades* in Mexico and PRAF in Honduras. *Oportunidades* integrates health, nutrition, education and income support features. A major service provided under the health and nutrition component is reproductive health, which allows women to plan their pregnancies, receive medical supervision during the crucial prenatal and post-natal periods, attain desired family size, and improve their children's health and nutrition. The PRAF program in Honduras integrates required school attendance and preventive health check-ups with income support for poor families.

Surprisingly, neither the Mexican nor the Honduran program includes an early childcare and development component. The results of our study strongly imply that such a component would leverage current interventions and significantly enhance the impact of these programs in breaking the cycle of poverty in these countries.

Other innovative programs introduced experimentally in a few countries include agricultural vouchers for very poor farmers to purchase modern inputs and technical assistance, conditional on school attendance by their children and health check-ups for all family members, including reproductive health services and nutritional education.

Integrated, family-focused government programs with income-enhancing opportunities for parents and basic services that enable families to build enough human capital to break out of the poverty trap will cost more than current programs. In view of the fiscal restrictions prevailing throughout the region and the political constraints to substantially reallocating budgetary outlays for basic social services to the poor, it is evident that resources are insufficient to extend such integrated programs to all or even most families that could benefit from them. Moreover, the poorer the country, the less resources available, and the greater the need in terms of the proportion of families trapped in poverty. Thus, regrettably, inclusion of families in the programs is inevitably selective. Of the various ways to ration access to the programs—such as first-come-first served, random selection, personal or political connections—we strongly favor a selection process targeted to those families whose needs and potential benefits are greatest. Recent advances in information technology and growing experience in the application of effective targeting methods are available to this end.

Investing in Early Childhood

Summary

Part One identified early childhood as a critical stage in the intergenerational transmission of poverty (ITP) and found investments related to early childhood care and development to be the most promising mechanisms to help people escape the poverty trap. Part Two now turns to discussing a basic menu of specific interventions and programmatic approaches to effect those investments. Box 1 shows how key investments in early childhood can be usefully linked to various stages in the poverty transmission cycle.

Family-focused anti-poverty programs were put forth in Part One as a broad strategy to combat the intergenerational transmission of poverty. This summary sketches a menu of more specific principles of, and approaches to, early childhood care and development investments, which are critical to implementing sound, family-focused anti-poverty strategies under varied settings and predilections.

Principles

In large measure because childbearing and child rearing are so deeply embedded in human nature, and so strongly fused with the cultural and

BOX 1. Early Childhood Care and Development Interventions at Different Stages of the Poverty Transmission Cycle

Stage	Investment
In the harsh economic and social environment of low-income communities, poor parents with little schooling and scant marketable skills . . .	
. . . tend to have children earlier in life, and have larger families, without the means or parenting skills to provide for their many children's developmental needs . . .	Life education and counseling to older children and adolescents, and reproductive health services to women can help parents delay pregnancy and plan their families.
. . . resulting in stunted children with an impaired ability to learn, leading to . . .	• Prenatal care and nutrition for mothers, along with good nutrition and health care for children in the early years, can improve conditions for the child's sound development. • Education and training in parental skills can help parents raise their children better. • Community education and training in safety, health, nutrition and child development strengthens parenting. • Developmental custodial care can help keep children safe and provide adequate stimulation to prepare them to learn in school.
. . . high rates of school failure (repeating grades or dropping out) and functional illiteracy leading to . . .	Educational and psychological support to underprivileged children during the initial school years will increase their chances of success in school and society.
. . . out-of-school and unskilled youth with scant marketable skills and poverty earnings . . .	Gender-informed social support and skills training for adolescents can expand the range of social and economic options available and reduce the risk of early motherhood, crime and violence.
. . . who mostly work at dead-end jobs or are engaged in illicit activities, tend to socialize with similar youth, resulting in early childbearing, becoming functionally poor parents who are likely to reproduce the poverty cycle . . .	

socioeconomic settings in which they occur, successful early childhood care and development programs defy rigid standardization across culturally and socioeconomically diverse communities. Sometimes those divides occur even within regions of a single country. Program designs, at least for the service delivery and client interphase, need to reflect these local features. Yet, there also are certain broad principles that can guide the approach to designing such programs, including the following:

- *Empower parents.* Undereducated mothers, fathers (and possibly other household members) must be empowered to become more effective parents and care providers, especially by enhancing their child rearing skills. The objective of investments in early childhood is to complement, not replace, the role of the family, and the most positive and long-lasting benefits of such programs happen when interventions combine support to the child's family with support to the child.
- *Address all unmet development requirements.* Programs should strive to ensure that all of the child's key custodial and developmental needs that would otherwise go unmet are attended to. Since child development is a multidimensional process and there are decisive synergetic relationships among these dimensions, support in key areas such as nutrition, health, basic skill development, social training and cognitively oriented education are mutually reinforcing. If a critical requirement such as nutrition goes (severely) unmet, successful development will not occur regardless of how fully all other requirements are satisfied. Like a three-legged stool, failure of a single leg leads to systemic failure.
- *Adjust to the socio-cultural context.* Unless early childhood care and development programs can identify the principal child-related needs of diverse communities and respond accordingly, they are likely to be regarded as extraneously imposed, and will not be entrusted with the community's children, especially the youngest. Consultation and participation are keys to success. Arriving with a standard package of protocols to address preconceived needs does not favor participation or achieving desired outcomes.
- *Intervene preventively.* For maximum cost effectiveness, the focus must be on preventive interventions at the early stages of the life cycle. Strong evidence suggests that the earlier that children and pregnant mothers begin benefiting from health and nutrition interventions, the greater the

impact on the child's physical and behavioral development, especially among extremely impoverished groups. Also, compelling medical and psychological evidence confirms that the period of early childhood, from conception through the first years of life, is critical to a child's social, emotional and cognitive development.

- *Make programs cost effective, financially feasible and sustainable.* This principle is discussed more fully later in this summary. Owing perhaps to the power of children's issues to stir emotions, it has been noted that the design and execution of children's programs are prone to be guided more by the heart than by objective calculation of cost-benefit and financial feasibility analysis, which are critical to the success of such programs. So it is worth stressing that unless early child care and development programs hew to reasonable standards of sound project analysis, design and management, especially concerning cost effectiveness, financial feasibility and sustainability, they are unlikely to contribute much to the goal of eradicating inherited poverty.

- *Focus program resources on households where the development outlook of the children would most likely be improved.* While the ideal and long-run objective is to provide universal coverage to *all* households with children that would benefit from high-quality early childhood care and development programs, fiscal or political constraints throughout Latin America generally render this unrealistic for the time being. A second-best policy prescription rooted in the utilitarian tradition thus seems warranted.

Approaches

Whether early childhood care and development programs focus on improving the nutritional status of pregnant women, enhancing parental skills, delivering services directly to children, or raising awareness about the importance of this issue in the community at large, their ultimate and common goal is to improve young children's capacity to develop and learn.

While all investments in early childhood should reflect core and guiding principles such as those above, there are various approaches that can be used to achieve the central goal of ensuring that children at risk fulfill their development potential. There are six notable approaches to early childhood care and development in addition to prenatal, peri-natal and mother-child health and nutrition services and preschool programs that normally are managed by ministries of health or education. The six are sketched below, followed by a more detailed discussion of two approaches particularly relevant to Latin America.

1. *Attending to children away from their home: the day care approach.* The day care approach can be in an institutional facility (center-based) or through arrangements in the caregiver's home, where one person cares for other people's children, and possibly her own (home-based).
2. *Supporting and educating parents and other family caregivers.* These efforts can be carried out through such programs as home visits, adult education or literacy courses, and child-to-child programs, as well as within nutrition or health education programs.
3. *Promoting child-centered community development.* The emphasis here is on the involvement and empowerment of entire communities in areas related to child safety and development.
4. *Institution-building.* The approach here is to strengthen public and civic organizations that can mobilize resources in support of child development.
5. *Strengthening national commitment.* By working to improve the legal, policy and regulatory framework related to children, this approach aims to create better conditions for young children and parents.
6. *Strengthening popular demand for early childhood care and development services.* This approach employs public awareness and social participation campaigns directed toward the general public, but particularly parents in poverty.

Applying the Day Care and Parental Support Approaches to Latin America[1]

Day Care Approach

Under the center-based modality of the day care approach, children attend programs in institutional facilities created or adapted for that purpose. In the industrialized countries, early childhood programs are often associated with formal preschools where training is conducted in a classroom-like atmosphere and children are prepared for primary school. A prime exam-

---

[1] This section is based on Myers (1995) and Young (1996).

ple is the French *école maternelle*, established in 1887 and today attended by almost 99 percent of all French children between ages three and six.

Such formal preschools, with their sophisticated pedagogic equipment and well-educated teachers, are too expensive to function on a significant scale in less-developed countries. In Latin America, such high-level formal preschool facilities are normally limited to private institutions that cater to higher income families. They are not a realistic option for publicly-financed and heavily-subsidized early childhood care and development programs in the region.

However, several Latin American countries have established formal child day care centers along the lines of the center-based modality—albeit on a much more modest level than the French version—for the children of middle- and lower-income households. The Colombian government in 1974 levied a 2 percent payroll tax (later increased to 3 percent) on all public and private employers to establish and operate public day care centers for children up to six years of age, incorporating health, nutrition and educational services. While the program is generally regarded as successful in terms of the children's physical and mental development, costs have been higher, and coverage, especially in rural areas, lower than originally envisaged. Some critics claim that an excessively top-down orientation has discouraged parental participation.

More recently, the Colombian government also established a home day care program, *Hogares de Bienestar*, that corresponds more to the home-based day care modality. The program provides training and support to the *madre cuidadora*, or childcare provider, in whose home the children are cared for. By design, the *madre cuidadora*, assisted by a trained specialist, is responsible for overseeing and directly providing the bulk of the work entailed in caring for up to 15 children from the neighborhood. Parents and other people from the local community are expected to contribute to the daily operation of these day care homes, including contributions of both labor and cash. Thus, in the early 1990s, the fiscal subsidy was set to cover less than 50 percent of total costs (Cardona, 1993).

While the center-based Colombian program provides reasonably high-quality early childhood care and development services for children, it was deemed too expensive by the government to be extended to the majority of children living in poverty. The home-based program is less expensive to the government, and, hence, broader coverage is fiscally and politically easier to extend. However, high quality standards have been more difficult to achieve in Colombia using this modality, although there have been home-based day care program in other Latin American countries that have managed to provide adequate care.[2]

Parental Support Approach

Parental support programs emphasize the enhancement of parenting skills among primary caregivers (mainly mothers, but also fathers or other adults in the homes of children at risk), and provide related support that reaches the child indirectly through the caregiver. The main purpose of parenting training is to strengthen the self-confidence of the parents and empower them with knowledge and skills that will enhance their ability to support their children's development. Training vehicles may include home visits, information and training in health and nutrition centers, and the use of videos and other media.

Several Latin American countries have undertaken parenting education initiatives. One of the more ambitious programs was launched in Mexico in 1992 with support from various United Nations organizations, as well as the Inter-American Development Bank. With a five-year horizon, the program was directed at the country's poorest families and entailed the employment and training of over 12,000 community educators, each of whom would work with around 20 families.

Radio and television have also been used to reach parents with information about child health and nutrition and related child development topics. In Venezuela, the *Proyecto Familia,* which started in 1980, has produced an impressive array of television and radio ads and programs, as well as slide presentations and films. In some countries, soap operas, cartoons and comic strips have been used to propagate the message (see Meyers, 1995, Chapter 7).

Measurable Benefits of Early Childhood Care and Development Interventions

Certain benefits of early childhood interventions begin to accrue immediately, while others can be reaped only in the longer term. Some benefits in

---

[2] See the essay in this book by Miguel Urrutia on Colombia. For examples from Venezuela and Ecuador, see Myers (1995, Chapter 6).

each category that are particularly important and amenable to empirical assessment are discussed in turn. Most of the empirical work on the benefits of early childhood developments has focused on the day care approach, which is reflected in the material summarized here.

Short-term Benefits

A benefit often registered quickly in the wake of center-based day care programs is increased labor participation and higher income for participating mothers. This benefit is rarely stressed as an explicit objective of such programs, which generally emphasize the benefits to the child. Nonetheless, by freeing time for the mother to work or study (especially outside the home), day care programs can be quite effective in increasing parental income in the short run or increasing skills leading to higher earnings and reduced poverty for the entire family.

Early childhood care and development programs can similarly free older siblings, especially girls, from childcare responsibilities at home, allowing them to remain in school instead.[3]

"Integrated" early childhood development programs—those that combine day care with psychosocial development, health and nutrition interventions, plus parental involvement—have been documented to be effective in improving the health and nutrition of children from impoverished households within one to two years after joining the program.[4] In circumstances of extreme poverty and its common correlate of preexisting child malnutrition, the qualification that the programs be integrated is essential. When programs consist of day care and feeding of children without much else, improvements in the nutritional status of such children tend to be minimal. In contrast, an evaluation of the Integrated Early Childhood Program *(Programa Integrado por Desarrollo Infantil—PIDI)* in Bolivia found that while 40 percent of a cohort of children enrolled in the program initially showed signs of stunted psychosocial development, the percentage was cut by half after one year in the program. After two years, the corresponding figure was down to 5 percent.

---

[3] For a survey of evidence, see Deutsch (1998, Chapter II).

[4] See Myers (1995).

Longer-term Benefits

The methodological requirements for reliably measuring the major long-term effects of early childhood care and development interventions are onerous. These include sample selection and control methods that tend to be unpopular with program administrators and entail nettlesome ethical issues. Then, most program graduates and control group members must be followed and interviewed over many years, ideally decades, to derive reliable measurements and robust inferences about causality. Not surprisingly, there are no major evaluations of this sort in Latin America. Many assessments of longer-term effects therefore rely on studies in industrialized countries, in particular the United States. Of these, the study of the Perry Preschool Program (see Box 2) is the most notable because of the length of the follow-up period of the children (from ages 3-5 in the mid-1960s to the present) and its scientific rigor.

While the Perry results show the range and depth of measurable benefits that can come from a well designed and implemented early childhood development program, the specific quantitative results may not be directly applicable to the circumstances in most Latin American countries. Another caveat in applying the results of such studies is that they are based on findings from purposefully, non-randomly selected programs, which are often characterized by careful design and strong commitment from key actors, probably enhanced by the knowledge that their program's performance is being observed—the so-called "Hawthorne effect." Quite often, these programs are also small and therefore likely to differ in significant ways from large-scale undertakings.

Findings for Latin America

With these caveats in mind, we synthesize below findings from certain studies based on what Latin American data is available. While falling short of the "gold standard" of evaluation methodology embodied in the Perry Preschool study, the data nevertheless appear sufficiently strong to support some important qualitative inferences.[5]

---

[5] Based on results reported in Myers (1995), Young (2001), van der Gaag and Tan (1998) and Part One of this book.

BOX 2. The High/Scope Perry Preschool Study: Compelling Findings on the Effects of an Early Childhood Care and Development Program

One of the best evaluations of the long-term impact of early childhood care and development programs is the High/Scope Perry Preschool Study (Schweinhart, 1993). Over a period of some 25 years, the study tracked two groups from Ypsilanti, Michigan: one that received a high-quality preschool program emphasizing active learning, and one that did not. The children, all African-American, lived in the same neighborhood in the 1960s. Researchers assessed the groups annually from age 3 to 11, at age 14-15, at age 19, and at age 27.

The researchers found that at age 27, the program group had:

- A significantly higher level of schooling;
- A significantly lower percentage of members who had received social services at some time in the preceding 10 years;
- Significantly fewer arrests, including significantly fewer drug-related arrests; and
- Significantly higher monthly earnings and home-ownership rates.

Data from the study suggest that returns on a preschool investment can be sevenfold. This finding was based on estimates of cost savings associated with reductions in the need for remedial education, in violence and crime, and in savings in other social programs. Using a more conservative methodology that excludes savings to potential crime victims, a more recent calculation re-estimates the corresponding returns to investment to be more than 4 to 1 (Karoly et al., 1998).

In addition, an evaluation of the effects on participating children of 11 early intervention programs found favorable and statistically significant results in all cases. A higher level of schooling attained by the program group was the most consistently observed positive result (found in six of the eight programs for which this effect was measured).

Compared to children from broadly the same geographical area and similar socioeconomic background, those that participated in early childhood care and development programs during the preschool years are more likely to enroll in primary school at the appropriate age; attain higher scores in standardized tests of mental and cognitive development around the time of primary school enrollment; progress normally across grades in primary and remain in school longer; and be evaluated in psychological tests as having better social skills, and by teachers as getting along better at school.

The last finding implies not only an important benefit to the better-behaved children themselves, but also the even more significant benefit to their classmates that results from an improved learning environment in the classroom and a happier teacher.

From the perspective of Latin American communities, perhaps the paramount social benefit from early childhood care and development programs for impoverished children is one that remains to be systematically measured for lack of suitable longitudinal data: the presumed effect of such programs on reducing the likelihood of antisocial and criminal behavior by these individuals when they become adolescents and beyond. However, from what information is available, the presumed effect on criminal behavior among early childhood development program graduates in Latin America is consistent with the very strong effect found in the Perry Preschool study in the United States. Moreover, it seems likely that if such a study were replicated in Latin American cities, the effect would turn out to be even stronger, considering the higher levels of early childhood deprivation among the urban poor in the region and the weaker police enforcement and deterrents there.

A second indirect piece of evidence supporting this contention is the widely reported observation that the vast majority of delinquent and criminal youths in Latin America have had highly deprived childhoods that included not only economic distress but also persistent abuse and neglect at home. Quality early childhood development programs, especially integrated programs that include interventions to address children's problems of abuse and neglect at home, could go far in improving the early childhood experience of children in poverty, and thus in eventually reducing the disturbingly high crime rates and public safety problems in so many Latin American cities.

Cost-Benefit Estimates for Two Programs in Latin America

Although no comprehensive cost-benefit analyses of early childhood care and development interventions have been conducted in Latin America that are based on real-time data—due in large part to the same onerous methodological requirements needed to measure long-term benefits—there is a scientifically rigorous study of the Bolivian Integrated Early Childhood Program (PIDI) mentioned earlier in this summary. The study assesses costs and benefits with a methodology that meets the criteria for suitable sample selection and controls and minimizes some limitations of not having longitudinal tracing of program graduates and randomly assigned composition of program and control groups (see van der Gaag and Tan, 1998).

The cost-benefit findings from both the Bolivian study and from another study on the Curumim Preschool Program in Brazil are encouraging. In Bolivia, based on rather conservative estimates of expected benefits, which include in the first instance only those associated with educational performance and consequent increased earnings of the participants, the estimated cost-benefit ratio of the PIDI program ranges between 1.38 and 2.07, depending on assumptions. When the expected program effect of lowering fertility is added, the cost-benefit ratio increases to the range of 2.38 to 3.06.[6]

In order words, for each dollar invested in the PIDI program, the benefits achieved were estimated to correspond to a value somewhere between double and triple that amount. This implies a very high rate of return that compares favorably with most development projects, even in such areas as physical infrastructure and industrial development.

The results from a study in Brazil on the costs and benefits of the Curumim Preschool Program for children in poverty in the slums of Belo Horizonte, the capital of the state of Minas Gerais, also showed favorable returns on program costs. The estimated rate of return for extended preschool services was in the range of 12.5 to 15 percent (see Paes de Barros and Mendonça, 1999).

Conclusions

Powerful and tested mechanisms are now available to tackle the intergenerational transmission of poverty in Latin America. Particularly promising are mechanisms that would intervene in the earliest stages of human life extending from conception to primary school age (6-8 years of age). It is at that point in a child's life that widespread shortfalls in meeting his or her minimum requirements for physical and emotional care—and just as importantly, psychological stimulation and nurturance—often lead to major and irreversible impairment of long-term human potential. It is also the opportunity for bringing to bear highly cost-effective intervention strategies, some of which have already been applied in demonstrably successful programs underway.

---

[6] Calculations of the cost-benefit ratio of the High/Scope Perry Preschool Project (see Box 2) indicate a value above 7.0, mainly as a result of gains in productivity in combination with lower repetition rates and lower public expenditures related to reduced welfare and crime.

As promising as such efforts may sound, unless the leaders of Latin America act decisively and soon, the problem of intergenerational transmission of poverty—with all its attendant and persistent economic, social and political repercussions—can be expected to worsen. The specific consequences for several Latin American countries where the social and political fabric is already highly stretched are difficult to predict, but could well disrupt both development efforts and political stability.

The remainder of Part Two of this book offers much to those leaders who are moved to respond vigorously to the challenge by presenting the lectures given at the seminar entitled "Breaking the Poverty Cycle: Investing in Early Childhood." Held during the Annual Meeting of the Inter-American Development Bank in Paris in March 1999, the seminar highlighted the magnitude and implications of the poverty cycle in Latin America and the Caribbean and the role of family factors in the dynamic of that cycle. The focus was on the central role of early childhood care and development interventions as a tool for interrupting the transmission of poverty across generations.

The Role of Early Childhood Investment in Development[1]

AMARTYA K. SEN

It can be argued that by viewing investment in children as part of the overall process of development, we develop a fuller understanding of the extensive reach and critical importance of investing in early childhood. It can also be argued that the comparative neglect of this important subject may be, to a great extent, the result of a limited and rather ad hoc view of the quality and implications of childhood. Seeing the issue within the rich perspective of developmental reasoning gives us a clearer appreciation, on the one hand, of the integral relation between childhood and adulthood, and on the other, of the interconnections between the lives of different persons and families who make up a total society. A developmental perspective can do greater justice both to the extensive interconnections that already exist as well as to integration that is still needed.

Development as Freedom

We can begin with the elementary question: What is "development"? The process of development can be seen as an expansion of human free-

---

[1] This essay and those that follow are taken from lectures given at the seminar, "Breaking the Poverty Cycle: Investing in Early Childhood," held in Paris in March 1999 (see IDB, 1999a).

dom.[2] The success of an economy and of a society cannot be separated from the lives that members of the society are able to lead. Since we not only value living well and satisfactorily, but also appreciate having control over our own lives, the quality of lives has to be judged not only by the way we end up living, but also by the substantive alternatives that we have. To illustrate the distinction, consider a person who lifts very heavy weights every day. In assessing the quality of life of this person, we have to examine whether he or she is doing this out of free choice (with other alternatives at hand), or is being forced to do this through the command of, say, some strong-armed slave-driver. It would make a difference.

Since the assessment of freedom can be sensitive both to what a person does and also to the alternatives he or she has, freedom provides a more inclusive perspective for judging human advantage, and through that, for assessing social success (Sen, 2002). This is the basic reasoning that provides the foundation of seeing "development as freedom" (Sen, 1999).

Focusing on human freedoms contrasts with narrower views of development, such as those that identify it with the growth of gross national product, or with the expansion of trade, or with industrialization, or with technological advance. Industrial, technological or GNP growth can, of course, be very important as a *means* to expand the freedoms of members of the society. But the freedoms that people enjoy depend also on other determinants, such as social and economic institutions (for example, education and health care facilities) as well as political and civil rights (for example, the liberty to participate in public discussions and scrutiny). Viewing development in terms of expanding substantive freedoms directs attention to the ends that make development important, rather than merely to some of the means that inter alia play a prominent part in the process.

Using this broad perspective, we can examine the particular role of investment in children. That role has many distinct features and aspects, and it is important to distinguish the different ways in which it can be important in enhancing human freedom and through that, advancing development. We are often told these days that we must take a "holistic" view, but in fact the subject calls also for analytical distinctions and empirical differentiations. The whole may be more than the sum-total of its parts,

---

[2] This perspective is discussed in Sen (1984). The demands and extensive implication of this approach are examined in Sen (1999).

but we have to be quite clear as to what the parts are before we appraise the whole.

Mortality as Unfreedom

The first and perhaps most elementary connection between childhood investment and development relates to child mortality. There are two issues here: (i) the empirical possibility of reducing child mortality (including infant mortality) through public and private investment, and (ii) the relevance to development of reducing child mortality.

Regarding the first issue, the existence of very strong empirical connections between investment and mortality reduction is amply confirmed by the observed regularity with which investments in such areas as nutrition, immunization and child care dramatically reduce the rate of child mortality when that rate is comparatively high. Indeed, worldwide experiences from Europe to Japan bring out how very effective even rather small investments in these fields can be.

If the issue of empirical connection is well established, then that of valuation should also be well recognized. Indeed, the evaluative relevance of mortality reduction in development performance is much more widely accepted now than it was even a decade or two earlier. As someone who has tried, for many years now, to argue in favor of the importance of mortality reduction as a constitutive part of development,[3] I am happy to report that opposition to that position seems now to be largely crumbling, at least at the practical level. A reflection of this shift is the fact that Mahbub ul Haq's *Human Development Reports*, which began in 1990 as a rebellion against accepted measures of development, have become an established part of development literature. Not everyone may yet agree on the importance of this perspective, and in some writings one still finds a defiant obduracy in the tendency to distinguish sharply between "human development," on the one hand, and simply "development," on the other—as if the latter takes

---

[3] In criticizing such measures as per capita GNP growth as the criterion of development (perhaps in some inequality-adjusted form), in the early 1970s I proposed a compromise; namely, that of having a "compound" criterion in which survival would be a crucial component along with income (Sen, 1973). It is, however, necessary to differentiate adequately between the normative bases of values of distinct concerns (including income and survival), rather than primarily seeking an immediately acceptable compromise. On this issue, see Sen (1974 and 1984).

note of the well-being of elephants and chimpanzees, in addition to humans. In the practical literature on development, however, increasing life expectancy and reducing mortality are now standardly taken as part and parcel of development accounting, broadly understood. No matter what we may think of such aggregate measures as the "human development index," which cannot but be defective (as any scalar representation of a complex vector of achievements must be), the subject matter of life and death is now well established in the development literature.

The issue is not just one of accounting acceptance, but also of conceptual clarity as to how development can be seen as a consolidated process of expanding human freedom, and why the reduction of child mortality (and the associated alleviation of child morbidity) can be placed solidly in the core of this integrated understanding. Avoidance of preventable mortality can be, in itself, a major contribution to the process of development, since premature death is a basic denial of the most elementary freedom of human beings. This is not only because we value (and have reason to value) living a normal life span, but also because most things that we want to do are helped by our being alive. One has to be "quick" rather than "dead" (as the medieval distinction put it) in order to accomplish many of the things we may value accomplishing. Living is not only fun; it is also a great facilitator of things we want to achieve.

Health and Survival of Children

This rudimentary point, which is obvious enough, is worth acknowledging explicitly. The issue is very broad, but it can be arbitrarily narrowed if our perspective were to concentrate only on poverty seen as low income. Indeed, the imperative to "break the poverty cycle" can be interpreted by some to be mainly an instruction to battle against the perpetuation of low incomes. But this interpretation would have the effect of significantly reducing the reach and relevance of the topic.

Child mortality, which still claims an astonishing number of lives, has to be seen as impoverishment in itself. Health care, public education, guarantees of food, and other measures that help to end the cycle of basic impoverishment must get a central place in an integrated approach. And the morbidities and sufferings associated with elevated child mortality also have claim to public attention. These afflictions also represent violations of the freedom of the very young to live in a way they can enjoy and treasure.

Childhood Quality and Adult Capabilities

Having noted the immediate relevance of the health and survival of children within a developmental perspective, we must turn to the connections between childhood and adulthood. In his engaging book, *The Twelve Who Survive*, Robert Myers plausibly argued that we cannot be concerned only with the prevention of child mortality, but must also focus on strengthening programs of early childhood development in order for those children to enjoy a fuller life. Enhancing the quality of children's life, which is influenced by such things as education, security, and the prevention of trauma, can be a crucially significant part of development.

Indeed, the quality of childhood has importance not only for what happens in childhood, but also for future life. Enrique Iglesias, the president of the Inter-American Development Bank, has noted that investments in early childhood "are important in their own right because they pave the way for a lifetime of improved health, mental and physical performance, and productivity. The right investments can go a long way toward minimizing and even preventing a host of other economic and social problems, ranging from juvenile delinquency to teenage pregnancy to domestic and social violence."

The capabilities that adults enjoy are deeply conditioned on their experiences as children. Here again we must distinguish between different elements in this interconnected picture. Investment in education and other features of childhood opportunities can enhance future capabilities in quite different ways. First, it can directly make adult lives richer and less problematic, since a securely preparatory childhood can augment our skill in living a good life. There is much social psychological evidence to suggest this.

Second, in addition to that "direct effect" on the capability to live a good life, childhood preparations and confidence also contribute to the ability of adult human beings to earn a living and be economically productive. The lives of adults are enriched through these earnings and economic rewards. Since that, in turn, influences the lives of their children and *their* future adult lives, there is a transmission problem. This relationship, which may be called the "indirect economic connection," vastly supplements the force of the direct effect of childhood quality on adult lives and capabilities. This connection is important in general, but it is especially serious in the specific context of female-headed households and female-maintained families (see Buvinić and Gupta, 1997; Buvinić, 1997). The indirect economic connection must be an area of concentrated research and action in the years to come.

The third connection is also indirect, but it relates to social linkages, which can extend beyond purely economic ones. Our ability to live with others, to participate in social activities, and to avoid social disasters, is also deeply influenced by the skills we form as children. We know something about these relationships on the basis of the existing literature, but this is a field in which much social and psychological research still needs to be done. Concerted action to enhance social capabilities deserves much more attention than it has received in the standard development literature.

There is also a fourth connection—a political one. The success of a democracy depends on the participation of citizens, and this is not a matter of just gut reaction but also of systematic preparation for living as active and deliberative citizens. These issues have been emphasized by various political observers such as Habermas (1979) and more recently Putnam (1993), among others (see also Chambers, 1996; Gutmann and Thompson, 1996; Bohman and Rehg, 1997.)

The childhood-adult connection has many distinct aspects. There is a need to develop a framework of interactive analysis that pays attention to the diverse elements in this relationship as well as to the manifest interconnections of these elements. According to Earls and Carlson (1993 and 1998a), the experience and quality of childhood have a profound impact on the capabilities of adults to live successfully in society. While Earls and Carlson illustrate these interconnections through their study of U.S. families (particularly in Chicago), there are general issues here that apply to other countries as well, not least in the rest of the Americas. We have a great deal to learn from each other.

Conclusions

I have commented briefly on a general approach to development that enables us to view the issue of investment in childhood from an inclusive perspective, as well as on some of the distinct elements in the adult-childhood relationship that have to be more fully seized for an adequate policy approach to this complex issue. It is important to see the diversities involved, covering our interest in the survival and quality of life of children, on the one hand, and the direct as well as indirect impact of childhood on the capabilities of adults to live worthwhile lives. The connections cover the direct skills associated with living as well as indirect effects through economic, social and political linkages. This is a subject of profound importance. The challenges involved are of interest to the entire world.

Bringing in New Actors

GRO HARLEM BRUNDTLAND

An important message needs to be brought to political deci-sion-makers: in the global development process, investing in health *matters*. While investing in health in general is a well-documented strategy for lifting populations out of poverty, investments in early child-hood are particularly cost-effective and represent a sound example of preventive public health policies.

The World Health Organization (WHO) actively reaches out to the inter-national financial institutions to create a joint quest for better health and better lives throughout the world. WHO and the development banks may have different roles, but they do not live in different worlds. It is imperative that all actors engaged in development work together toward common goals.

Reliable overviews of the global burden of disease show that the leading causes of mortality or disability traditionally have been respiratory infec-tions, diarrhea and birth-related conditions. The leading risk factors are malnutrition, poor water and sanitation. There has been no significant change in the rankings of causes of mortality, disability or risk since 1965 or even earlier. But even if the top causes of child mortality remain the same, the levels for most of them have dropped significantly. Overall child mortality rates and life expectancy have greatly improved, and more children survive the first five years of their lives than ever before.

Still, it is in child mortality where social inequalities have become most visible. Most of the unfinished health agenda at the doorstep of the 21st century is explained by the persistence of childhood illnesses that we have the tools to combat. Yet the application of those tools to all has failed because of social inequality and inequitable health systems. The end result is that improvements in child health over the past few decades have not been shared by all. This is why causes of deaths that should no longer be a worldwide problem continue to occupy the top ranks. It also means that we have more children than ever to take care of. The improvements in science and public health that allow so many more children to survive their first years have handed us a new responsibility: Having secured children their survival, we must ensure that they can have a healthy and stimulating childhood that will prepare them for the challenges of life, and enable them to contribute to the social and economic development of their countries and communities.

Investing in early childhood means investing in poverty prevention. We have known for a long time that poverty breeds ill health. What some have long suspected, but which only recently has become evident, is that it works both ways. That is, ill health perpetuates poverty and is at the root of the poverty cycle. And, clearly, the way to break the intergenerational poverty cycle is to focus on children. The world is making some headway in addressing these issues. Strong and cost-effective tools are now available to improve the lives of the youngest children. Integrated approaches to children's needs that recognize the importance of early childhood care for survival, growth and development have changed the way we look at strategies for helping children living in poverty.

Areas that require attention are cognitive stimulation and the psychosocial factors that affect child development. But the underlying foundation for normal mental development is the absence of serious disease. A child weakened by repeated attacks of diarrhea or malaria will benefit less from cognitive stimulation and psychosocial interventions. Preventing or arresting the repeated assaults of illness on a young child is therefore an integral and fundamental part of development efforts.

Nutrition is a key factor in these efforts. The effects of nutrition not only on growth and physical development, but also on cognitive and social development, are well documented. A malnourished child is more vulnerable to disease, and his or her cognitive development will be in peril, especially during the first three years of life. Stunted physical growth is closely linked to reduced mental development.

Intervention in childhood care and development to break the poverty cycle need to start long before birth. Approximately 10 percent of the global burden of disease is associated with failures to address reproductive health needs. Many of these problems stem from adolescents becoming parents far too early. The individual and societal costs of the 600,000 deaths from maternal causes and 7.6 million perinatal deaths every year are staggering. Failing to ensure that young people have the knowledge, skills and services they need to make healthy choices in their sexual and reproductive lives costs us dearly.

Investing in reproductive health is an investment in future health and development. Reproductive health, nutrition and combating common early childhood diseases must take a central place in any childhood development program. Other development activities can spring from this. Health, nutrition, and cognitive and social stimulation, as well as education, are complementary issues that lend themselves to cooperation across professional boundaries. A child's day is not compartmentalized into health, nutrition, education and the like. We must ensure that health and education, nutrition and social activities blend into one protective and nourishing environment for the child.

One of WHO's contributions to early childhood care and development is the strategy for Integrated Management of Childhood Illness (IMCI). The strategy is a product of lessons learned during the fight against childhood diseases. Many previous and disparate strategies to combat single diseases in children often missed opportunities, resulted in redundant efforts, and gave mothers advice that was confusing or too narrow.

IMCI is important because it focuses on the youngest children (from birth to five years old), who traditionally have been the most difficult to reach. It is also important because it uses existing infrastructure as a starting point: local health workers are given training and support to assist children and parents. A child brought to a clinic with diarrhea will be treated for that complaint, but will also be checked for acute respiratory infections and other diseases and receive a nutritional assessment. In one integrated consultation, the child will be vaccinated, and the mother informed about breastfeeding, other aspects of nutrition, and other preventive measures such as the importance of mosquito nets in malaria prone areas. These efforts to improve health worker practices are complemented in the IMCI strategy by improvements in health infrastructure and by focused efforts to change key family and community practices.

IMCI is a relatively new strategy, yet some measures of success are already in evidence. In Uganda, one of 109 countries worldwide that have adopted the IMCI strategy to date, one baffled mother coming out of a health station in a small village last year asked suspiciously whether there had been a major pay increase for nurses, since the health workers now actually talked to her at length and showed unusual concern for her child. In Brazil, one of the 19 Latin America and the Caribbean countries that use IMCI, data from a research study suggest that nutritional counseling for mothers in poor rural areas by health workers trained in IMCI has pretty much eliminated the drop in weight that had been normal for babies in the transition period from mother's milk to ordinary household food.

The strategy also emphasizes that no opportunity to immunize a child should be missed. Childhood immunization is an area of considerable achievements. The proportion of the world's children who are vaccinated has risen from less than 5 percent in the 1970s to around 80 percent in 1999. More recent and detailed estimates suggest that it was around 73 percent in 2000. But maintaining coverage at these levels is an ongoing task, and extending this basic service to all children is an unmet challenge. There is still a long time lag between the introduction of new vaccines into the developed world and the availability of those same vaccines to the world's less privileged children. Creative financing mechanisms are part of the solution to these outstanding issues. The key is teamwork across disciplines and agencies.

Real societal changes require a multifaceted approach that incorporates education, nutrition, health and social components, as well as economic considerations. For example, once the economic implications of environmental degradation were understood, the environment was transformed from being a cause to becoming a real societal issue of interest to major players. The same is true for health.

Thus, in order to achieve progress and results in childhood development and reduce the intergenerational transmission of poverty, we need working partnerships. Often the best partnerships are those that are forged between unorthodox entities. When people with vastly different backgrounds come together with a shared purpose, creativity is released and expertise is used in innovative and constructive ways. To this end, the World Health Organization is cooperating closely with the World Bank and the International Monetary Fund, as well as with the regional development banks.

Economic crises in Asia and Latin America have brought home the need to protect and strengthen social sector activities and ensure low-cost and universal health and education systems for all. "Trickle-down" economics does not work on its own. Although this fact may be obscured during good economic times, it becomes glaringly apparent during recession and crisis. Nowhere is the need for intervention greater than in ensuring that children get the childhood to which they have a right. Research now shows that there are important economic benefits to be reaped from investing in early childhood.

But interventions need to be cost-effective. It need not cost a lot to make substantial improvements in children's conditions. But poorly designed programs can easily become failures, wasting meager public resources and making it harder to convince decision-makers next time around that child-focused programs are of value.

When prime ministers and finance ministers are told that early childhood development is also their business—that wise investments yield real results—then they will listen in a different way and consider changing their traditional priorities. When they see that there are sound and cost-effective strategies, and that they are backed by world-renowned expertise, then there is real hope that they will actually allot money for them. We have the expertise, we have a growing number of cost-effective strategies, and we have a willing and competent financier. In short, we have what it takes to improve conditions for the children of the Americas and the rest of the world.

The Impact of Early Childhood Intervention on Economic Growth and Equity

MIGUEL URRUTIA

In the early 1970s in Colombia, a group of economists learned of research by nutritionists, some of it carried out in Colombia, that showed that malnourished children became seriously impaired physically and intellectually, and that the harm produced might not be reversible. As a result, the government's development plan for 1975-78, whose objectives were poverty reduction and better distribution of income, included an infant nutrition program as a strategic objective. The program—which was called "Closing the Gap," a reference to the policy of reducing inequality—analyzed the benefits of an infant nutrition plan in terms very similar to those that are now used to justify early childhood intervention projects (Departamento Nacional de Planeación, 1975). It was based on several key assumptions:

- An adequate diet has a beneficial impact on the health of children and mothers, and therefore decreases the call on funds from the public health system.
- The elimination of malnutrition positively affects the productive physical and intellectual capacity of the labor force in present and future generations.

- An appropriate nutritional intervention improves the productivity of educational investment by increasing the study and absorption capacity of students, as well as by reducing school dropout rates.
- Since a large proportion of Colombia's food is produced by smallholders, a food supplement program benefits the poorest agricultural producers by increasing the demand for foodstuffs. The food coupon initiative included a nutrition education component and was implemented through health posts and preschool centers.

The nutrition program was presented to the World Bank, which approved a loan for its implementation in record time. At the same time, the Inter-American Development Bank and the World Bank approved loans for ambitious integrated rural development projects that were to increase food production and, in turn, improve nutrition.

The evaluation of the nutrition plan was quite positive, but the food supplement program was discontinued during the fiscal crisis of the 1980s (Uribe Mosquera, 1983a and b). Clearly, the benefits of the program had not created powerful stakeholders to defend it. The integrated rural development programs were fairly successful, unlike the experience in many other countries, and these programs continued, with ups and downs, for 20 years. The programs turned out to be more popular politically, in part because community participation mechanisms were included in the projects.

During the same period when this range of programs was implemented, the government in 1974 passed a 2 percent payroll tax to finance the establishment of day care centers at or near places of employment of working mothers. The tax, which later was increased to 3 percent, produced (and still produces) substantial revenues and freed the Family Welfare Institute *(Instituto de Bienestar Familiar),* which supports the day care centers, from budget cuts during times of fiscal adjustment. The day care center program has expanded substantially and has also traditionally provided nutrition supplements.

The first lesson that can be drawn from the implementation of this plan is one of political economy. Why do some early childhood interventions survive and others not? The Colombian experience suggests that the design of the programs must consider the creation of groups ready to defend them. The Planning Department coordinated the various activities of the nutrition program with the many executing agencies involved, but none of the agencies considered the program to be its own. An added element was that the Planning Department is an institution made up of high-level technocrats with high turnover and many objectives. It is certainly not the type of bureaucratic institution that depends on a specific program to receive a budget or for institutional continuity. In fact, the idea to discontinue the food supplement program came from the head of the department after a change in government.

The childcare program, on the other hand, was given independent resources and was in charge of a permanent bureaucracy whose main objective is child development. Children and mothers of poor families have little political clout, but a dedicated bureaucracy can successfully defend social programs, as long as care is taken that the bureaucracy does not absorb the bulk of resources to pay for its own salaries, as has happened with the teacher's union in Colombia and other countries. Employed women are also more likely to organize to defend day care centers (which they need in order to work) than pregnant or lactating mothers are able to organize in defense of food supplements.

The nature of the nutrition problem also changed rather rapidly in Colombia. Uribe Mosquera (1987) has shown how malnutrition shifted over the short span of a decade (1972-81) in Colombia from being predominantly a rural phenomenon to being primarily an urban problem. Economic growth and improvements in income distribution had the effect of lowering malnutrition from 40 percent of the poorest segments of the population in 1971 to 10 to 20 percent in 1981. By that same year, the risk of malnutrition had become higher in urban than in rural areas. Food insecurity went from being 70 percent rural in 1972 to 60 percent urban in 1981. These changes required major strategic adjustments in the nutrition programs, but those changes were never implemented.

The New Consensus on Early Childhood Intervention

Even during implementation of the nutrition program, there were other more integrated childhood intervention programs being carried out in Colombia that yielded impressive results in terms of health and school performance of the participating children. Of particular note was the health and day care program implemented in Cali by the *Fundación de Investigaciones de Ecología Humana* (McKey et al., 1978). The problem with the program, however, was that it had a high cost per child. Generally speaking, early childhood care and development programs are expensive, so it is important that their design ensure a high benefit/cost ratio.

The most effective programs aimed at early childhood appear to be those that combine nutrition, health care and cognitive development components. Programs that integrate health and school performance are much closer to what today is considered the most advisable type of early childhood intervention programs.

The renewed interest in early childhood is stimulated by a growing body of evidence from a diverse array of disciplines that confirms, once again, that early childhood, from conception through at least age 3, is critical to a child's development. Research and clinical work have found that the experience of the infant and young child provides the foundation for long-term physical and mental health as well as cognitive development (Karoly et al., 1998). Early childhood interventions are formal attempts by agents outside the family to maintain or improve the quality of life of youngsters, starting with the prenatal period and continuing through entry into school.

The effects of health care, nutrition and mental stimulation on children's mental and emotional growth—as reflected in their ability to master ever more complex activities as well as their physical growth—are synergistic and cannot be broken up into separate domains. Integrated programs, therefore, seek to address all of children's basic needs. In addition to food, protection and health care, childcare programs must also provide affection, intellectual stimulation, supportive human interaction, and opportunities and activities that promote learning (Young, 1996).

If improved life chances only occur as a result of actions in all these areas, it is clear why early child development interventions can be quite costly. Given limited government budgets, such programs will not be implemented unless the benefits exceed the costs by a substantial amount. It is useful, therefore, to list some of the benefits of these programs.

The most immediate benefit of early child development interventions is to facilitate the participation of low-income mothers in the labor force. This reduces poverty, improves nutrition, and reduces fertility. While the benefits for children will only be evident after many years, longitudinal studies show that the influence of early environment on brain development is long lasting. Evidence from some studies shows that infants exposed to good nutrition, toys and playmates had measurably better brain function at 12 years of age than those raised in a less stimulating environment. This is particularly true for participants in these programs that come from the poorest households. Participating children have higher school enrollment rates and less grade repetition, and fewer of them drop out of school. Not surprisingly, evaluations of some U.S. programs in which participating children were subsequently monitored for more than two decades reported that their incomes at age 27 were much higher than those of nonparticipants (Karoly et al., 1998). Childcare centers allow girls to go to school instead of staying at home to care for their younger siblings. In a survey of U.S. programs, the Rand Corporation was able to identify four that attempted to measure crime and delinquency among youth when they were followed at older ages after having participated in early childhood care and development programs. In all four cases, there was a lower incidence or seriousness of juvenile offenses for those in treatment versus control groups (Karoly et al., 1998). By itself, this finding would justify early childhood care and development programs in Colombia and other Latin American countries where crime is a major problem.

Quantifying the Benefit/Cost Ratio of Early Childhood Development Interventions

To justify early childhood development programs, evaluation methodologies should be designed that allow for the quantification of program benefits. Unfortunately such methodologies have seldom been included in these programs. In particular, control groups have not been identified and followed for comparison purposes with the children who participate in the programs, particularly in Latin America.

As mentioned, however, some programs in the United States have provided sufficient information on participating children and control groups. In addition to its finding of lower crime rates, the Rand surveys of the literature on these programs identified substantial benefits for participating children as well as resulting savings for the government in terms of lower use of welfare funds and special education resources.

In the U.S. programs, these savings were higher than program costs, but they may be lower in developing countries, where there are fewer welfare programs. However, an evaluation of Bolivia's Integral Program for Early Child Development (*Proyecto Integral de Desarrollo Infantil—PIDI*) estimated benefit/cost ratios of between 2.38 and 3.10 (van der Gag and Tan, 1998), implying a very high rate of return on the investment. Most of the measured benefits can be explained by the improved level of schooling for PIDI participants, which in turn generates more highly productive workers. The increase in labor force participation of the mothers also increases family income significantly.

The lack of adequate evaluation procedures, however, does not allow the identification of those early childhood intervention programs that yield the most benefits. Given the high cost of the programs, it is crucial that their design allow for such evaluation so that the most efficient combination of interventions can be adopted.

Low-cost vs. Costly Integrated Programs

From 1982 to 1986, Turkey's Early Enrichment Project, in an effort to identify the optimal combination of home- and center-based custodial and educational day care services, studied the effects of different approaches on preschool children. While educational day care got the best results in all measures of psychosocial development, children whose mothers had received training and outside support also showed significant gains (Young, 1996). Since the latter system is less costly, it is more attractive for cash-strapped governments. On the other hand, the benefit/cost ratio may be lower and there may be less promotion of equal opportunity for all children. In Turkey, it was decided to use the cheaper model (parental education) instead of center-based care.

Although less desirable from the point of view of improving income distribution and creating equal opportunities for all, the lower cost programs may still have high rates of return on investments in human capital. Such seems to be the case of the Bolivian PIDI project, which consists of informal home-based day care centers where children receive nutrition, health and cognitive development services.

The environment of the home-based programs may be, however, less than optimal. In the Colombian *Hogares de Bienestar* program, day care is provided in the homes of volunteer mothers. It appears that these homes often have inadequate sanitation, dirt floors and too small a space per child, and lack sufficient educational and play stimuli for the children. In addition, day care volunteers do not recognize the signs of malnutrition, nutrition supplements are inadequate, and there is very little health training of day care helpers and mothers. Those deficiencies may seriously diminish the benefits to the children (Instituto Colombiano de Bienestar Familiar, 1997).

It is interesting that the agency in charge of the program resisted for many years an independent external evaluation, which when done, identified the problems described. On paper, however, the program looked impressive. It covered 745,100 children up to 6 years old, and 84 percent of the target group was from the poorest two of six economic strata. An inadequate evaluation procedure makes it difficult to say whether the program produced tangible benefits. What has been shown, however, is that the better-quality day care centers do produce better results than the average for the program in terms of nutrition, health, and psychosocial behavior (Instituto Colombiano de Bienestar Familiar, 1997).

In most social programs, high costs result from salary payments. It is a mistake, then, to skimp on physical infrastructure and didactic and cooking materials for day care centers. Investment in such centers would guarantee a better environment for the child, and yet most of the cost of the program would continue to be payments to volunteer mothers and the administrative apparatus of the program.

Another interesting finding of the evaluation of the Colombian program was that the health and nutritional status of children was highly dependent on the prenatal care received by the mother, which is not a component of the early childhood intervention program. The nutrition program of the 1970s had such a component in the form of food coupons distributed by health centers at the time of prenatal visits. The coupons were a good incentive for mothers to go to the health centers. The nutritional supplements and health education and care provided on the visit helped avoid low weight babies. It would seem that a coordinated approach through health and day care centers might be an effective way to reach children from birth to 6 years old.

In summary, although the best early childhood intervention programs may be those that are well targeted and integrated, it may be possible to increase coverage by designing more participative programs with volunteer or semi-volunteer helpers. It is important that salaries for staff not represent too great a proportion of available revenues.

Despite the emphasis that has to be put on avoiding large expenditures, it should be mentioned that the cost of equalizing access to education, including preschool education and health services, is estimated by some at about 1 percent of GNP for most Latin American countries. This is a small price to pay for breaking the vicious cycle of the intergenerational transmission of poverty.

Conclusions

In many Latin American countries, progress in poverty reduction and improvements in income distribution have been very slow. One of the major causes for this has been the exceedingly slow progress toward universalizing education. Despite investing a substantial proportion of GNP in public education, many Latin American countries have school enrollment rates that are lower than might be expected. According to UNESCO, while Colombia spent 3.5 percent of GNP on public education, Hong Kong spent 2.8 percent and Korea 3.7 percent. Yet in Colombia, only 61 percent of an age cohort finishes the 5th grade, compared to 100 percent completion in Korea and Hong Kong.

Clearly, if better access to education is a precondition for improving income distribution and reducing poverty, then measures must be taken to increase enrollment and retention rates, and to lower grade repetition. All evidence suggests that the best way to achieve these positive changes is through early childhood intervention programs of the sort described here. Universal coverage in primary and secondary education not only improves income distribution; economic growth models also show that increased education is a major determinant of rapid economic development.

Early childhood intervention programs provide other valuable benefits, such as greater opportunities for women, higher female labor force participation rates, decreased fertility, and better health. An additional benefit of great value is a probable decrease in the incidence of crime and antisocial behavior, which can be attributed to better interpersonal relations within the family and less domestic violence.

Still unclear is the type of early intervention that is most effective. Clearly, the effects on a child's potential are better if the program includes health and nutrition monitoring, day care, and preschool education. But such a program can be quite expensive, and most developing countries have limited fiscal resources. There is, therefore, a need to determine which program components produce the desired benefits at a reasonable cost, particularly in terms of school enrollment and retention.

Determining an adequate program design will require that all projects include a methodology for following up on participating children and comparing them to a control group. The resulting benefit-cost analysis can help determine the type of programs that should be carried out in the future.

Defining the technical aspects of the programs is important because, in the absence of some degree of scientific consensus on what components the programs should include, there will be implementation delays. When the Colombian nutrition plan was being prepared, there were continuous discussions on whether to attack protein or calorie deficiencies, and about which type of food supplements to provide. Determining which agency should be in charge of which service, and how to target the programs to the poor, were exhausting processes.

International experience has now provided answers to many of the technical problems concerning the design of early childhood intervention programs. But serious evaluations can help to determine the degree of acceptable trade-offs between lower quality and less professional services delivered at low cost, and higher quality but more expensive programs. Clear research results will strengthen arguments about the value of investing in programs for vulnerable children, help determine which programs are the most effective, and head off many delays in design and implementation.

How to Invest in Early Childhood Care and Development

ROBERT G. MYERS

There are a number of arguments that make a convincing rationale for investing in early childhood care and development: human development, economic gain, social equity, social values, social mobility, social change and human rights.

Human development: Scientific research demonstrates forcefully that the first years of life are critical in the formation of intelligence, personality and social behavior throughout the lifecyle.

Economic gain: Society benefits economically from early child development through increased production by the parents or caregivers whose time is freed to earn and learn, and by the children themselves when they become adults. Investing in early childhood also saves money over the long haul in terms of programs for health, education, crime and others.

Social equity: Providing children with a "fair start" in life makes it possible to moderate distressing social and economic inequalities. It helps children and families escape from poverty, and provides more equal possibilities for women.

Social values: Humanity transmits its values through children, and this process begins in the earliest years of life. The process of perpetuating and preserving the desired social and moral values that are the basis for responsible citizenship needs to begin with young children.

Social mobilization: Children provide a rallying point for social and political actions that benefit the broader community and that can build consensus and solidarity.

Social change: The increasing survival of vulnerable children, changing family structures, migration to cities, increased participation of women in the work force, and other changes affect child care, socialization and educational styles and needs. These changes require new responses.

Human rights: Children have a right to develop to their full potential.

This compelling combination of arguments for investing in early childhood care and development suggests it is now time to move on from asking "why invest?" to such questions as: "How should we invest?" and "What works?" The sections that follow address these questions by setting out strategies and guidelines that experience and evaluation have suggested should lead to effective outcomes.

What Can We Do? Six Strategies

What needs to be done and what will work depends, of course, on particular circumstances. The situation of children in a rural extended family, whose livelihood is subsistence agriculture, will be very different from that of children in a single parent, female-headed urban household, where the mother works in the informal sector or in a factory. Child rearing practices in an indigenous culture will differ from those in a *mestizo* culture. Children of migrant workers face different conditions than those who live permanently in one place. The situation will differ depending on whether or not a family has access to clean water and health services, there is a prevalence of diseases such as malaria, there is enough food to put on the table, the community is isolated or accessible by road, and so forth. Both poverty and child development needs take on a different tone in these varied settings.

Because conditions can vary so widely, there is no unique and universal formula for creating an early childhood care and development program. Nevertheless, the process of child development itself provides some common elements that must be considered in any program. Child development is multi-faceted, involving physical, mental, social and emotional dimensions. Therefore, programs must include components for health and nutrition as well as education and socialization. The priority given to these different dimensions will vary among settings. For example, if basic nutrition and health conditions seem to be met, but there is little attention to educational stimulation, emphasis may need to be placed on getting parents to talk more to their child, or on providing alternative settings where a child will receive the kind of stimulation that a family is not providing. The overriding principle, however, should be that the child receives integral attention. The development of a child is a continuous process beginning before birth. Therefore, regardless of the setting, we need to be concerned about the child from conception onward. This means that programs must be concerned with mothers during pregnancy just as they are with the child at later stages. Child development occurs as a child, each with his or her particular genetic make-up, interacts with the surrounding environment. Therefore, programs should try to change harmful elements of that environment just as they try to change the child.

The environment with which a child interacts, and which influences how a child develops, has various levels. A child develops within the contexts of family, community and society, with established institutions such as the school and church, and in a culture with certain beliefs and practices. Each of these contexts provides a possible roadmap for investments in early childhood. There are six different but complementary strategies that can be adopted.

Strategy 1. Attending to Children Away from the Home

The immediate goal of this center-based direct approach is to enhance child development and learning by creating an environment that complements (and sometimes substitutes for) the home. This is the strategy that most frequently comes to mind when people talk about early childhood programs. Within the public sector, the most common response is to think in terms of formal preschool programs directed to children in the year before they enter primary school. However, there are other forms of care and early education that may be as, or more, important than a formal preschool. Attention can and should be provided at earlier ages. A center-based approach can involve informal as well as formal preschools; government, community-run or business-related childcare centers and crèches; day care arrangements (in which a person cares for a group of children in her own home); organized playgroups; and attention to mothers and children in health centers.

There are any number of examples of early childhood development systems that function well, with benefits for both children and families. An extraordinary system of center-based early education in place in France entails virtually 100 percent coverage for children from age 3 onward. In Sweden, over 50 percent of all children from ages 1-6 are in full-day, high quality child care centers; another 14 percent are in home day care arrangements; and yet another 6 percent are in a preschool group.

An example in Latin America is the privately operated, community-based center in Mexico City run by Doña Concepción Arista. Women from the community have been trained to handle a Montessori curriculum that was modified to take local culture into account. They provide a stimulating experience in active learning, appropriate to a child's level of development, for the 100 plus children enrolled. Parents can enroll their children for only three hours a day or for a longer period depending on their needs.

Approximately one-fourth of all children in low-income areas of Mexico City are enrolled in childcare or pre-school centers classified as private or community centers, either because there is no access to public services or because the quality of the community centers is judged to be better. Unfortunately, these centers, which serve an important social function, often have financial problems because they cannot charge parents what it costs to run the program. In large part, such programs continue to function because energetic and dedicated women like Doña Concepción are willing to work for the good of others.

Strategy 2. Supporting and Educating Parents and other Family Caregivers

This approach aims to educate and enable parents and other family members in ways that improve their care for and interaction with the child. Family members are part of a child's social and emotional environment and are also responsible for the physical environment that affects a child's development. Family caregivers can be educated through programs of home visits; in adult education or literacy courses; within nutrition or health education programs; through child-to-child programs; by using mass media; or as part of a general community development strategy.

In European countries, support to parents is provided through such means as direct child subsidies or tax exemptions, liberal maternity benefits, work leave programs, and housing subsidies. These approaches are not likely to be as feasible in most of Latin America, both for financial reasons and because of their potential effect on population growth. But they can form part of much longer-term thinking.

An illuminating example of a successful parental education program comes from Turkey, where a national program was established to help mothers become better caregivers and teachers of their children. The program, which developed over 15 years, involves collaboration between a non-governmental organization (the Mother-Child Education Foundation) and the government (through its Department of Adult Education and the Social Welfare and Child Protection Agency). It is built around weekly group meetings with mothers that are designed to increase their sensitivity to children's social and emotional needs, and to help foster their cognitive and psychosocial development in the home environment. The program has been extended to more than 50 provinces and has reached over 40,000 families. Evaluations have consistently shown lasting benefits to the children during their primary school years as well as positive changes in the mother-child relationship, in the mother's attitude, and in relationships with the father.

Strategy 3. Promoting Child-centered Community Development

Child-centered community development places emphasis on addressing community conditions that may adversely affect child development. This strategy takes the welfare of children as an entry point for fostering community initiative, organization and participation in a range of inter-related activities to improve the physical environment, knowledge and practices, and the organizational base of community members, thereby benefiting children and the community at large.

In Colombia, a project called PROMESA operated by the *Centro Internacional de Educación y Desarrollo Humano* (CINDE) combines the child-centered, community-based approach with a parental education approach. The project began in four villages along the isolated Pacific coast of Colombia, where most families live in extreme poverty, eking out a living from fishing or subsistence farming. The children often fail to finish primary school, and malaria is rampant. The project began by working with

100 mothers, 25 in each village, who met weekly to discuss with a *promotora* how they might create a better environment to improve the health and intellectual development of their children. The project quickly moved from a focus on the use of toys that foster cognitive development to a broad set of health and nutrition actions involving others in the community, and then on to income-generating projects. All of this was done in the name of the healthy development of young children. Some of the mothers took on the role of "multipliers." The program also led to the establishment of community organizations and collaborative actions involving other NGOs, the national and state government, and the community, with some financial support from international organizations. Over a period of 20 years, the project grew from 100 to 7,000 families.

A somewhat similar process was developed on the northern coast of Colombia by the *Proyecto Costa Atlántica*, a program of the *Universidad del Norte* to provide comprehensive attention to young children in selected communities. The needs of children served as a stimulus to community organizations to resolve common problems affecting the community in general. The project was carried out in collaboration with the government's Family Welfare Institute, which imparted a local tone to a national program by adapting it to local needs and facilitating community management. This program led to improvements in literacy, health and housing, as well as improved childhood development and school performance.

These two projects illustrate many of the programming principles that will be set out in the next section, including an integral and multi-faceted approach focused on marginalized families; the importance of community participation, adjusting to cultural differences, and starting where people are in terms of their needs and knowledge; the need to take a long-term perspective; an inter-generational approach benefiting adults as well as children; and working in partnership. Along with the broader Colombian Home Day Care Program and others, these programs also illustrate the idea that coverage can result from the sum of various efforts, adjusted to local circumstances and employing different models.

Strategy 4. Strengthening Institutional Resources and Capacities

The many government and civic institutions involved in early childhood care and development need adequate financial, material and human resources to do a proper job. This strategy may involve training or technical assistance, or experimentation with innovative techniques and models to improve the available technology.

Strategy 5. Improving the Legal, Regulatory and Policy Frameworks

This strategy might involve reforming a national constitution, passing new laws, establishing national committees, or incorporating an early childhood dimension into regular planning and reporting processes.

Strategy 6. Strengthening Public Demand and Awareness

Directed toward affecting the broad cultural ethos that influences child rearing, this strategy concentrates on the production and distribution of knowledge in order to create awareness and demand in the population at large and promote social participation.

Programming Principles for Early Childhood Care and Development

Whether an early childhood program is center-based or directed toward parents or a child-centered community program, there are a number of principles or guidelines that, experience suggests, should be followed if investments are to have maximum effect.

Place projects and programs within a larger policy and programming framework. Often, successful early childhood care and development programs are inserted in, or lead out to, broader social actions in such areas as health, education, employment, women's rights, housing, or even crime prevention. It is useful, therefore, to look for logical ways in which existing poverty programs can incorporate an early childhood development component, as well as examine how freestanding care programs can be established.

Focus on high-risk families. In general, this means giving priority to low-income and socially marginalized families and groups who live in rural areas, are of indigenous origin, or work in the informal sector. This priority derives from studies suggesting that, in most cases, children who are at the greatest disadvantage can benefit the most from interventions. It is also consistent with equity concerns.

Be participatory and community-based. This means involving families and communities in meaningful ways as partners in project planning, implementation and evaluation. It involves building on and reinforcing what families and communities are doing right, rather than just identifying what is wrong and trying to fill in with "compensatory" programs.

Be flexible and adjust to different sociocultural contexts. Early childhood care and development is closely tied to culture as well as to economic and social conditions. What to do and how to do it depends very much on the context. This leads to the uncomfortable, but inevitable, conclusion that there is no one formula to follow. Fortunately, however, we can draw upon accumulated experience in a wide variety of contexts.

Seek quality. What constitutes quality in early childhood care and development? The most important element of quality resides with the people who are selected and trained to be caregivers and educators. Following an established and proven curriculum also enhances quality. Safe, clean and healthy environments are also crucial, but these can be created without constructing fancy or large facilities.

Take an intergenerational approach, benefiting other members of the family, especially mothers. One important corollary of this principle is that attention should be given to whether proposed programs place additional burdens on mothers and other family members, or help to free up time for them to earn, learn and develop themselves. In most formal preschool programs, for instance, hours are short and inflexible, focusing on the education of children without taking into account the needs of parents. This means that the programs do not help women to enter the labor force in productive jobs.

Seek cost-effectiveness. Without dwelling on this principle, it is important to note that it depends as much on how effectiveness is defined as it does on costs.

Work together. Co-participation, co-responsibility or partnership are essential not only because early childhood care and development is of such importance and magnitude that we need to combine resources, but also because involving governments, social organizations, private enterprise and communities can help to improve the design and implementation of programs.

Incorporate monitoring and evaluation into programs from the outset. It is critical to know how to make adjustments and whether the program has accomplished what it set out to do. We need also to increase our knowledge of what works better in order to improve future programs.

Costs and Financing

The cost of an early childhood care and development program depends on such choices as the coverage desired; the range of services provided; the characteristics of the population served (age, healthy vs. handicapped, malnourished); the location of that population (isolated rural communities vs. urban areas); the child-to-staff ratios; and the particular model or strategy chosen (center-based, home visits, mass media approaches). The diversity of early childhood programs is reflected in a comparably broad range of (unit) costs that, according to one study, vary from $28 to nearly $3,400 per child per year.

Programs Need not be Expensive to be Effective

This point was brought home forcefully during a visit to a rural center in Karnataka in India, where I witnessed what might be called the Indian rope trick. An extraordinary woman there, Indira Swaminathan, invented her own cognitive curriculum. Among 25 items in her "cognitive kit" was a three-meter rope to work her magic—hardly a costly item. Arriving at a one-room village preschool center, we found 40 children who had been arranged in a circle, most of whom sat inertly and with rather blank stares. I watched as Indira tied the ends of the rope together and then placed it in the hands of the group of assembled children, now connected together in the circle by the rope. She then took her place in the circle, sitting between two of the children and began a series of routines that helped children learn the concepts of up and down, to identify the shape of a circle and a triangle, and to work as a group. This was fun and, within moments, children who had been outside the circle began to clamor to be part of the game. Eyes began to shine and minds began to work.

How Can Early Childhood Care and Development Programs be Financed?

Financing must come from a combination of institutions and groups, including (1) the government (from general revenues or linked to special taxes such as social security, a payroll or property tax, a tax on license plates, or from special activities such as lotteries or, as in Mexico, running a national pawn brokerage); (2) parents and families (through the payment of fees or contributions in kind or in time); (3) community and other social groups (through their specific budgets or by organizing donations of time or money); (4) the private sector (by paying taxes, but also by engaging in philanthropy and by companies using their own budgets for social ends in enlightened self-interests); and (5) international institutions (by providing funds on a grant or loan basis).

What Different Sectors Can Do

Public Sector

- Increase the budgetary priority given to early childhood care and development.
- Establish national councils to help integrate program lines and to re-examine laws pertaining to the care and development of young children.
- Support mass education campaigns directed toward parents.

Civil Society

- Identify and provide technical support community programs for early childhood care and development.
- Provide needed analyses of the status of children and evaluations of ongoing programs.
- Promote, organize and operate early childhood programs.

Private Sector

These suggestions go beyond paying corporate taxes or contributing to social security, which in some countries includes the right to childcare. There are many possible ways to get involved and build partnerships. Thinking first in terms of their own employees, businesses might:

- Establish and run centers within their own workplace or provide a child-care subsidy to employees so that their children can attend centers run by others. This can increase employee satisfaction and reduce absenteeism.
- Where not provided through the formal social security system, lobby for a program of benefits that includes leave to care for newborns.

- Offer flexible time to employees to participate in parental education programs provided within or outside the workplace (this has been done in Turkey).

In several of these cases, it would be logical to think that a firm might be exempted from child-related social security payments if it established its own program. But looking beyond one's own immediate employees, it is possible to imagine other roles for the private sector that would improve a company's image and hence its business. For instance, businesses might:

- Organize or contribute to philanthropic efforts benefiting children, either directly by a business or through contributions (in cash or in kind) to, for instance, a social development fund designated to support community-based early childhood programs.
- "Adopt" a center in an area where the business is located or where employees live.
- Provide organizational and administrative assistance on a pro bono basis to community-based and privately run centers, seen as small social businesses, helping them with accounting systems and perhaps with fundraising.
- Participate in information campaigns by donating advertising talent or time, or by including child development messages in flyers or billings.
- Partner with public service agencies in supporting early childhood care and development programs.

Conclusions

Investing wisely in early childhood care and development is a great challenge, but there is knowledge and experience to draw upon. If we combine that knowledge and experience with will, dedication and persistence, we can anticipate enormous benefits to children, their families and communities, and society in general. Today's children will be responsible in the 21st century for achieving economic growth with social justice, for halting the devastation of our environment, and for building a world in which neighbors and nations can live together in peace. Providing them today with early experiences that are healthy and satisfying will give them the roots and wings they will need to be the dreamers, builders and leaders of a better tomorrow.

Investing in Children: The Role of the State in Unequal Societies

NANCY BIRDSALL

Investing in children is key to the kind of development that improves people's lives by improving their capabilities. This essay addresses the question of why governments should intervene in the lives of small children, who are clearly the responsibility of families. It also looks at the difficult politics of investing in children.

Why should the state intervene at all in early childhood development? The answer is because there is an even a more compelling truth behind the dry statements of economic logic about the high returns to investing in children and the presence of capital and other market failures that may imply lower investment by families than they or society would like. In unequal societies, with high levels of poverty and high concentrations of income, interventions to help children are win-win measures that are good for both social equity and economic efficiency.

Most Latin American countries have enthusiastically embraced a broad set of market reforms—including fiscal rectitude, monetary discipline, privatization of state enterprises and trade liberalization—designed to create a competitive, or level, playing field. These reforms in essence increase the value of assets such as land, physical capital, information, and, most of all, education. Those who already have these assets come to the market game equipped to play. Whether they do well or not depends on their skill and energy. But some players, including all too often the children of the poor, arrive at the game without the assets and other equipment necessary to play well. They may not even have the proper uniform that is a prerequisite for taking the field. If they do manage to enter the game, they are likely to lose, and may eventually abandon altogether the effort to play.

Early childhood intervention programs fundamentally are about providing all children the opportunity to enter the game with a fair chance to win—that is, with the proper equipment and training to ensure that competition is fair. In the unequal societies of Latin America, there will otherwise be a smaller pool of eligible players, fewer teams, and a less productive league. A level playing field even at age 6 may already represent an unfair contest for children who are malnourished and have never had a book read to them. Ideally it is parents who ensure that their children get a fair chance at schooling and jobs by investing time, energy and money early on. But if parents and family cannot or do not do so, it is in society's interest to step in. Otherwise there will be too few players and too little competition for the local league to compete in the global contest that today's international markets constitute.

In the short run, the market reforms that are spurred by and reinforce the global integration of markets—which ultimately represents a key to rapid growth in the region—can make the game even more unfair. This is especially true in Latin America, where the poor are especially poor and where the distribution of land and education remains so unequal. Because the poor lack those productive assets, market reforms will not necessarily help them. Conventional reforms need to be supplemented with aggressive policies and programs to increase the assets of the poor in order to ensure that they can exploit new market opportunities. Among other things, that means putting a premium on early childhood intervention programs. The more poor families there are, and the more unequal the society, the greater the logic for the state to channel tax and other public resources to child intervention programs.

The Difficult Politics of Investing in Children

If public investment in early childhood is such a good idea that reconciles efficiency and equity, why isn't there more of it, and how might more be ensured? Three reasons account for why there is not more such public investment. First, the costs of early childhood development programs are immediate and obvious; the benefits come later with less certainty. Even the heralded Head Start program in the United States still fights for funds, although over the years its size and visibility have helped insulate it from the budget axe and, in addition, state and local governments can and do step in when the federal government cuts back.

The second reason for this lack of public investment in children is that controversy and uncertainty about the technical issues—what to do, what is most cost-effective, what is the right mix of inputs in what conditions?—make extracting resources from the political system difficult. A simple message is easier to sell. This is not to say that the technical issues are not real. Should childcare be publicly financed in neighbors' homes or in larger facilities with better conditions and better-trained staff? What is more cost-effective, concentrating scarce resources on prenatal care or on nutritional supplements for infants? No one any longer questions the idea of spending public resources to send children to primary school, so there is political space for debates about class size and teacher training. This is not yet the case for many early childhood programs.

The third reason is realpolitik. Families are diffused and disorganized, particularly if they are poor. They are busy with jobs and small children. Everyone who pays taxes expects some day to be old, and perhaps to need the safety net provided by public funding for old age programs. But no taxpayer will ever again be a child. Colombia's day care program survived, but its nutrition program did not. The former built up a big bureaucracy that fought for survival and the latter did not. Creating an entrenched bureaucracy, however, can be self-defeating. It may help a program survive, but that does not necessarily mean that the program benefits the children, their families or society, particularly if programs become vehicles to support the providers rather than deliver services to clients. Other means for creating a benign lobby for children and children's programs have to be found.

How, then, can advocates of these programs obtain sustainable political support in the real world of real political choices? The following five notions are worth considering.

First, make creating a political constituency for child programs a consideration in the design of programs. Some would say cost-effectiveness and technical efficiency should trump political appeal. But in cost-benefit terms (and because of the economic logic referred to above), investments in children outrank many other investments. Though the ideal set of cost-effective inputs is not clear, there is a range of approaches and inputs that meet the cost-benefit test and are worth "selling" politically. Consider this example: adding pre-kindergarten to all public schools as a universal program, publicly financed not only for the poor, but for all. In Washington, D.C., pre-kindergarten was first offered as an option in most schools about 20 years ago. Within a decade parents wanted it in all schools. Virtually all 4-year olds now attend school, whereas before only the children of better-off households attended (private) programs. Though not legally mandated, pre-kindergarten has become a social norm and there is no way the public resources it absorbs can be politically withdrawn.

Second, get steady, sustainable earmarked public resources. Economists do not like earmarked taxes, but even they admit that we live in a second-best world (given market failures) where apparent truths no longer necessarily apply. The 2 percent payroll tax instituted in Colombia to pay for early childhood care, which was later raised to 3 percent, is a sign of political success built on the bedrock of the steady financing that the tax provided. As a result, that country has been able to maintain its day care program during times of fiscal adjustment.

Third, welcome and build on the initiatives of small community groups, civil society and, of course, local governments. This must be done regardless of how difficult the potential relations and how initially incompetent these potential partners might be. Even if not pioneers of technical or administrative efficiency, these are political partners in a good cause.

Fourth, create powerful and demanding consumers, with legitimate expectations for good quality and sustained programs. Empowered consumers are the most effective political proponents of a public program. Consumers by definition require choice—otherwise they are "beneficiaries." This implies that programs should be demand-driven and face competition, which in turn implies that not all programs for childcare, prenatal care, and so on need to be directly supplied by government. Government can allow and even encourage provision by private providers in the not-for-profit and profit-making sectors. When purchasing day care and other services, poor households need public subsidies to make them effective consumers (subsidies should be equivalent to cash— "vouchers" is the term used in the case of schools). This kind of approach—multiple providers and vouchers for poor households—has already been shown to work well in Argentina, Chile and Paraguay in the case of vocational training. Why not try it for programs that constitute investments in young children? Making more poor households discerning consumers is a sensible way to inform and educate all of society about the logic and benefits of early childhood programs. Government's role is then to provide information, standards and evaluation of alternative providers so that consumers can make informed choices.

Fifth, create new providers (such as mothers as microentrepreneurs) whose business success relies in part on public subsidies for their poor clients. At least one of the program options for preschool childcare should include the kind of home-based program developed in Colombia, in which women who are prepared to manage day care in their own homes receive training and a minimal amount of assistance to meet physical standards (ideally via credit programs). They are then periodically "accredited" as eligible to provide services. On the one hand, it may be that the level of care at given costs can be better in more institutionalized settings. On the other, parents as consumers can benefit from the ability to choose between different care options (based on convenience, proximity, flexibility in hours of operation, etc.) One obvious choice is the home of a neighbor, friend or relative that the system essentially upgrades by making it part of a larger system that ensures minimal information and standards. Politically, there are advantages to having providers who benefit from the public subsidies while participating in a competitive, choice-based system.

Fortunately the overall contours of realpolitik are changing. Democracy, decentralization and an increasing number of civil society groups in the region are all ingredients for increasing effective political demand for public investments in children.

To conclude, a simple point should be made. In the unequal societies of Latin America, where market reforms are creating new opportunities, the investments with the highest return are those that make those opportunities more accessible to more people. Investing in children makes new opportunities more accessible. It thus guarantees a future that is both more fair and more prosperous for all.

Bibliography

Aldaz-Carroll, Enrique, and Ricardo Morán. 2001. *Escaping the Poverty Trap in Latin America: The Role of Family Factors.* In *Cuadernos de Economía* 38(114): 155-91.

Astbury, J. 1999. *Promoting Women's Mental Health.* Geneva: World Health Organization.

Balderston, L.B., A.B. Wilson, M.E. Freire, and M.S. Simenon. 1981. Malnourished Children of the Rural Poor—The Web of Food, Health, Education, Fertility and Agricultural Production. Boston: Auburn House.

Becker, Gary. 1975. *Human Capital.* Chicago: University of Chicago Press.

_____. 1991. *A Treatise on the Family.* Cambridge: Cambridge University Press.

Becker, Gary, and Gregg Lewis. 1973. On the Interaction between Quantity and Quality of Children. *Journal of Political Economy* 81 (March-April).

Behrman, Jere R. 1998. Social Mobility. Concepts and Measurement in Latin America and the Caribbean. Presentation at the CSED/IDB Workshop on Social Mobility. Brookings Institution, Washington, D.C.

Behrman, Jere R., and Barbara L. Wolfe. 1987. Investments in Schooling in Two Generations in Pre-revolutionary Nicaragua: The Roles of Family Background and School Supply. *Journal of Development Economics* 27: 395-419.

Behrman, Jere R., Nancy Birdsall, and Miguel Székely. 1998. *Intergenerational Schooling Mobility and Macro Conditions and Schooling Policies in Latin America.* Inter-American Development Bank Office of the Chief Economist Working Paper 386. September.

Behrman, Jere R., Yingmei Cheng, and Petra Todd. 2000. Summary of Report on the Impact of the Bolivian Integrated PIDI Preschool Program. Department of Economics, University of Pennsylvania. March. Mimeo.

Behrman, Jere R., and Paul Taubman. 1990. The Intergenerational Correlation between Children's Adult Earnings and their Parents' Income: Results from the Michigan Panel Survey of Income Dynamics. *Review of Income and Wealth* 36: 115-27.

Birdsall, Nancy. 1980. A Cost of Siblings: Child Schooling in Urban Colombia. *Research in Population Economics* 2: 115-50.

Bohman, J., and W. Rehg (eds.). 1997. *Deliberative Democracy.* Cambridge, MA: MIT Press.

Buvinić, Mayra. 1997. Women in Poverty: A New Global Underclass. *Foreign Policy* 108.

⸻. 1998. Costs of Adolescent Childbearing: A Review of Evidence from Chile, Barbados, Guatemala and Mexico. *Studies in Family Planning* 24(2) June: 201-09.

Buvinić, Mayra, and Geeta R. Gupta. 1997. Female-Headed Households and Female-Maintained Families: Are They Worth Targeting to Reduce Poverty in Developing Countries. *Economic Development and Cultural Change* 45(2).

Buvinić, Mayra, Andrew Morrison, and Michael Shifter. 1999. *La violencia en América Latina y el Caribe. Un marco de referencia para la acción.* IDB Sustainable Development Department Technical Paper SOC-110, Washington, D.C.

Buvinić, Mayra, Juan P. Valenzuela, Temístocles Molina, and Electra González. 1992. The Fortunes of Adolescent Mothers and Their Children: The Transmission of Poverty in Santiago, Chile. *Population and Development Review* 18(2).

Cardona, Carlos C. 1993. *Home-based Community Day Care and Children's Rights: The Colombian Case.* UNICEF, Innocenti Occasional Papers, Florence, Italy. May.

Castañeda, Tarsicio. 1979. *Fertility, Child Schooling and the Labor Force Participation of Mothers in Colombia, 1977.* Chicago: University of Chicago.

⸻. 1997. Health Sector Reform in Colombia: Issues, Options and Lessons. World Bank, Washington, D.C. Unpublished.

⸻. 1998. The Design, Implementation and Impact of Food Stamp Programs and Other Direct Subsidy Programs in Developing Countries. World Bank, Washington, D.C. Unpublished.

Castañeda, Tarsicio, and Enrique Aldaz-Carroll. 1999. The Intergeneration Transmission of Poverty: Some Causes and Policy Implications. Paper presented at the IDB seminar on Breaking the Poverty Cycle: Investing in Early Childhood, Paris, March.

Chambers, S. 1996. *Reasonable Democracy.* Ithaca, NY: Cornell University Press.

Chiswick, B.R. 1988. Differences in Education and Earnings across Racial and Ethnic Groups: Tastes, Discrimination, and Investments in Child Quality. *Quarterly Journal of Economics* (August): 571-97.

Cornia, Giovanni Andrea, Richard Jolly, and Frances Stewart. 1987. *Adjustment with a Human Face.* Oxford, UK: Oxford University Press.

Departamento Nacional de Planeación. 1975. Para cerrar la brecha. Plan de desarrollo social, económico y regional 1975-78. Bogota, Colombia.

Deutsch, Ruthanne. 1998. *How Early Childhood Interventions Can Reduce Inequality: An Overview of Recent Findings.* Inter-American Development Bank Sustainable Development Department, Best Practice Study POV105, Washington, D.C.

de Vylder, Stefan. *Macroeconomic Policies and Children's Rights.* Klippan, Sweden: Save the Children.

Duryea, S., and M. Székely. 1998. *Labor Markets in Latin America: A Supply-Side Story.* Inter-American Development Bank Office of the Chief Economist Working Paper Series 374, Washington, D. C.

Earls, F., and Maya Carlson. 1993. Towards Sustainable Development for American Families. *Daedalus* 122.

_____. 1998a. Adolescents as Collaborators: In Search of Well-being. Harvard University. Mimeo.

1998b. El bienestar de la infancia hacia el año 2000: Logros y limitaciones. In ECLAC, *Panorama Social de América Latina.* Santiago de Chile: ECLAC.

Economic Commission for Latin America and the Caribbean (ECLAC). 1998. *Panorama social de América Latina 1997.* Santiago: ECLAC.

_____. 2000. *Equity, Development and Citizenship.* Mexico City. April. Mimeo.

Evans, Judith L., et. al. 2000. *Early Childhood Counts. A Programming Guide on Early Childhood Care for Development.* Washington, D.C.: World Bank Institute

Felitti, V.J., R.F. Anda, D. Nordenberg, D.F. Williamson, A.M. Spitz, V. Edwards, M.P. Koss, and J.S. Marks. 1998. Relationship of Childhood Abuse and Household Dysfunction. *American Journal of Preventive Medicine* 14(4): 245-58.

Fields, G. 2003. Long-Term Economic Mobility and the Private Sector in Developing Countries. Online at: http://www.ilr.cornell.edu/extension/files/20021210025851-pub1148.pdf

Furstenberg, Frank, et al. 1988. *Adolescent Mothers in Later Life.* Cambridge, UK: Cambridge University Press.

_____. 1999. *Managing to Make It: Urban Families in High-Risk Neighborhoods.* Chicago: University of Chicago Press

Gaviria, Alejandro, and Carmen Pagés. Patterns of Crime Victimization in Latin America. Inter-American Development Bank, Washington, D.C. Mimeo. October.

Gertler, P., and P. Glewwe. 1989. *The Willingness to Pay for Education in Developing Countries: Evidence from Rural Peru.* Living Standard Measurement Study Working Paper no. 54. World Bank, Washington, D.C.

Glewwe, Paul. 1995. *Who Is Most Vulnerable to Macroeconomic Shocks? Hypotheses Tests Using Panel Data from Peru.* Washington, DC: World Bank.

Gomez de León, J. 1998. Dimensiones correlativas de la pobreza en México. Elementos para la focalización de programas sociales. Latin American and Caribbean Economic Association.

Gottschalk, Peter, Sara McLanahan, and Gary D. Sandefur. 1994. The Dynamics and Intergenerational Transmission of Poverty and Welfare. In Sheldon H. Danziger, Gary D. Sandefur, and Daniel H. Weinberg (eds.), *Confronting Poverty: Prescriptions for Change.* New York: Harvard University Press.

Gutmann, A., and Dennis Thompson. 1996. *Democracy and Disagreement.* Cambridge, MA: Harvard University Press.

Habermas, J. 1979. *Communication and the Evolution of Society.* Boston: Beacon Press.

Heise, L., M. Ellsberg, and A. Gottemoeller. 1999. Ending Violence Against Women. In *Population Reports,* Series L, no. 11, John Hopkins University School of Public Health. December.

Holmqvist, Göran. 1999. Latin American Crime and the Issue of Inequality. Institute of Latin American Studies at the University of Stockholm. Mimeo. November.

Instituto Colombiano de Bienestar Familiar (ICBF). 1997. Primera encuesta del Sistema de Evaluación de Impacto Hogares Comunitarios de Bienestar Social. IBCF, Bogota.

Instituto Cuánto. 1991. *Ajuste y economía familiar, 1985-1990.* Lima: Instituto Cuánto.

Inter-American Development Bank (IDB). 1998. *Para salir de la pobreza. El enfoque del Banco Interamericano de Desarrollo para reducir la pobreza.* Special report by the IDB Poverty Unit, Washington, D.C. Online at: http://www.iadb.org/sds/doc/pov%2DSantiagoS.pdf

_____. 1999. *Facing Up to Inequality in Latin America. Economic and Social Progress in Latin America, 1998-1999 Report.* Washington, D.C.: IDB.

_____. 1999a. Breaking the Poverty Cycle: Keynote Addresses by Gro Harlem Brundtland and Amartya Sen 11/99. SOC-114.

Karoly, Lynn A., Peter Greened, Susan Everingham, Jill Houbé, Rebecca Kilburn, Peter Rydell, Matthew Sanders, and James Chiesa. 1998. *Investing in Our Children. What We Know and Don't Know About the Costs and Benefits of Early Childhood Interventions.* Santa Monica, CA: Rand Corporation.

Jencks, C., et al. 1972. Inequality: A Reassessment of the Effects of Family and Schooling in America. New York: Basic Books.

Lam, David, and Suzanne Duryea. 1998. Effects of Schooling on Fertility, Labor Supply, and Investments in Children, with Evidence From Brazil. *Journal of Human Resources.*

Larrain, Soledad. 1997. *Relaciones familiares y maltrato infantil.* Santiago: UNICEF.

Lewis, M., et al. (eds). 1979. *The Child and its Family: The Genesis of Behavior.* New York: Plenum.

Lillard, Lee, and Rebecca Kilburn. 1997. *Assortative Mating and Family Links in Permanent Earnings.* Working Paper Series 97-02. Labor and Population Program.

Lindstrand, Ann, et al. 1999. *Global Health—An Introductory Textbook.* Stockholm: Karolinska Institutet.

Lloyd, C.B. 1994. Investing in the Next Generation: The Implications of High Fertility at the Level of the Family. In Overseas Development Council, U.S.-Third World Policy Perspectives no. 19, Washington, D.C.

Lloyd-Sherlock, Peter. 2000. Failing the Needy: Public Social Spending in Latin America. *Journal of International Development* 12(1) January.

Londoño, Juan Luis, and Rodrigo Guerrero. *Violencia en América Latina: Epidemiologia y costos.* IDB Office of the Chief Economist Working Paper Series R-375, Washington, D.C. August.

Londoño, Juan Luis, and Miguel Székely. 1997. *Persistent Poverty and Excess Inequality: Latin America 1970-1995.* IDB Office of the Chief Economist Working Paper Series 357, Washington, D.C. September.

López, Ramon. 1995. Determinants of Rural Poverty: A Quantitative Analysis for Chile. World Bank Latin America and the Caribbean Regional Office, Washington, D.C.

López, Ramón, and Carla della Maggiora. 2000. Rural Poverty in Peru: Stylized Facts and Analytics for Policy. In Ramón López and Alberto Valdés, *Rural Poverty in Latin America: Analytics, New Empirical Evidence and Policy.* New York: St. Martin's Press.

López, Ramon, and Alberto Valdés. 2000. *Rural Poverty in Latin America: Analytics, New Empirical Evidence and Policy.* New York: St. Martin's Press.

Maynard, Rebecca A. (ed.). 1996. *Kids Having Kids: A Robin Hood Foundation Special Report on the Costs of Adolescent Childbearing.* New York: The Robin Hood Foundation.

McKey, H., et al. 1978. Improving Cognitive Ability in Chronically Deprived Children. *Science* 200 (April).

McGuire, Judith. 1998. Social Exclusion and Malnutrition in Latin America. World Bank, Washington, D.C. Unpublished.

Mehrotra, Santosh, and Richard Jolly (eds.). 1997. *Development with a Human Face. Experiences in Social Achievement and Economic Growth.* Oxford: Clarendon Press.

Morán, Ricardo, et. al. 1997. The Uses of Cost Analysis in Early Child Care and Development (ECCD) Programs. IDB Social Programs Division, Washington, D.C. Mimeo. February.

Morán, R., and J. Haefeli. 1998. Interrupting the Intergenerational Transmission of Poverty: The IDB and Early Childcare and Development. Inter-American Development Bank Sustainable Development Department, Social Development Division. Mimeo.

Morán, Ricardo, and Robert Myers. 1999. ECCD Guide: A Toolkit for Early Childhood Care and Development. Inter-American Development Bank Sustainable Development Department, Washington, D.C. On the web at www.iadb.org/sds/SOC/publication/publication_53_524_e.htm

Morley, S., et al. 1998. La utilización de fondos de inversión social como instrumento de lucha contra la pobreza. Inter.-American Development Bank Sustainable Development Department, Washington, D.C. Mimeo.

Morrison, Andrew R., and Maria L. Biehl (eds). 1999. *Too Close to Home: Domestic Violence in the Americas.* Washington D.C.: Inter-American Development Bank.

Morrison, Andrew R., and Maria Beatriz Orlando. 1997. El impacto socioeconómico de la violencia doméstica contra la mujer en Chile y Nicaragua. Document from the conference on Violencia doméstica en América Latina y el Caribe: Costos, programas y políticas, Inter-American Development Bank, Washington, D.C.

Myers, Robert. 1995. *The Twelve Who Survive.* Ypsilanti, Ml: High/Scope Press.

Paes de Barros, Ricardo, and Mendonça, Rosane. 1999. *Costs and Benefits of Pre-School Education in Brazil.* Rio de Janeiro: Institute of Applied Economic Research (IPEA), Division of Social Studies and Policies.

Patrinos, Harry A. 1998. *The Costs of Discrimination in Latin America.* Human Capital Development and Operations Policy Working Paper. World Bank, Washington, D.C.

Psacharopoulos, George. 1995. *Building Human Capital for Better Lives.* Washington D.C.: World Bank.

Psacharopoulos, George, and Ana Maria Arriagada. 1989. The Determinants of Early Age Human Capital Formation: Evidence From Brazil. *Economic Development and Cultural Change* 37(4): 683-708.

Psacharopoulos, George, and Harry A. Patrinos. 1994. *Indigenous People and Poverty in Latin America: An Empirical Analysis.* Washington, D.C.: World Bank.

Putnam, R.D. 1993. *Making Democracy Work: Civic Traditions in Modern Italy.* Princeton: Princeton University Press.

Raczynski, Dagmar. 1987. *Chile.* In Cornia et al., *Adjustment with a Human Face.* Vol. 2. Oxford, UK: Clarendon Press.

Rogers, B., T. Sanghvi, P. Tatian, J. Behrman, M. Calderón, S. Crelia, and M. García. 1995. Food and Income Subsidies and Primary Schooling in Rural Honduras: An Evaluation of the Impact of the Bonos (BMJF) and PL 480 – Title II School Feeding Programs. USAID/ADAI/LAC/HNS.

Rosales Ortiz, J., E. Loaiza, D. Primante, A. Barberena, L. Blandón Sequeira, and M. Ellsberg. 1999. *Encuesta nicaragüense de demografía y salud.* Instituto Nacional de Estadísticas y Censos, Managua.

Schultz, T. Paul. 2001. *Why Governments Should Invest More in Educating Girls.* Economic Growth Center Discussion Paper No. 836. In *World Development* 30(2): 207-25.

Schweinhart, Lawrence J., et al. 1993. *Significant Benefits: The High/Scope Perry Preschool Study Through Age 27.* Monographs of the High/Scope Perry Educational Research Foundation, no. 10. High/Scope Educational Research Foundation, Ypsilanti, MI.

Selowsky, Marcelo. 1978. *The Economic Dimensions of Malnutrition in Young Children: A Survey of the Issues.* Washington, DC: World Bank.

Sen, Amartya. 1973. On the Development of Basic Income Indicators to Supplement the GNP Measure. *United Nations Economic Bulletin for Asia and the Far East* 24.

_____. 1974. Informational Basis of Alternative Welfare Approaches: Aggregation and Income Distribution. *Journal of Public Economics* 3.

_____. 1984. *Resources, Values and Development.* Cambridge, MA: Harvard University Press.

_____. 1988. The Concept of Development. In H. Chenery and T. N. Srinivasan (eds.), *Handbook of Development Economics.* Amsterdam: North Holland.

_____. 1999. *Development as Freedom.* New York: Knopf.

_____. 2002. Rationality and Freedom. Cambridge, MA: Harvard University Press.

Simmons, J., and L. Alexander. 1980. Factors which Promote School Achievement in Developing Countries: A Review of the Research. In J. Simmons (ed.), *The Education Dilemma.* Oxford: Pergamon Press.

Skoufias, Emmanuel, and Bonnie McClafferty. 2001. Is Progresa Working? Summary of the Results of an Evaluation by IFPRI. The International Food Policy Research Institute (IFPRI), Washington, D.C. Mimeo.

Solon, G. 1992. Intergenerational Income Mobility in the United States. *American Economic Review* 82(3): 393-408.

Uribe Mosquera, T. 1983a. The Right to Food: A Critical Review. In *Seminar on Food Aid, Report of the World Food Programme.* Government of the Netherlands.

_____. 1983b. The Political Economy of Colombia's PAN. In Pinstrup-Andersen, *The Political Economy of Food and Nutrition Policies.* Washington: International Food Policy Research Institute (IFPRI).

_____. 1987. Revaluación de la inseguridad alimentaria en Colombia. *Coyuntura económica* 17(1) April.

Vandemoortele, Jan. 2000. *Absorbing Social Shocks and Reducing Poverty. The Role of Basic Social Services.* New York: UNICEF.

van der Gaag, Jacques, and Jee-Peng Tan. 1998. *The Benefits of Early Child Development Programs. An Economic Analysis.* Washington, D.C.: World Bank.

van der Gaag, J., and D. Winkler. 1998. Children of the Poor in Latin America and the Caribbean. Paper presented at the World Bank's Annual Conference on Development in Latin America and the Caribbean, Washington, D.C.

van de Walle, Dominique. 1998. Targeting Revisited. *The World Bank Research Observer* 13(2) August.

Velez, E., E. Castaño, and R. Deutsch. 1998. An Interpretation of Colombia's SISBEN: A Composite Welfare Index Derived From the Optimal Scaling Algorithm. Inter-American Development Bank, Washington, D.C. Unpublished.

Walker, E., A. Gelfand, W. Katon, M. Koss, M.V. Korff, D. Bernstein, and J. Russo. 1999. Adult Health Status of Women with Histories of Childhood Abuse and Neglect. *American Journal of Medicine* 107(4): 332-39.

Warren, J. R., and R. M. Hauser. 1997. Social Stratification Across Three Generations: New Evidence from the Wisconsin Longitudinal Study. *American Sociological Review* 62: 561-72.

Wolfe, Barbara L., and Jere R. Behrman. 1982. Determinants of Child Mortality, Health and Nutrition in a Developing Country. *Journal of Development Economics* 11: 163-93.

World Bank. 1998a. Business Partners for Development. Finance Private Sector Development, World Bank Group. Online at: http://www.bpdweb.org/contact. htm

———. 1998b. Girls' Access, Persistence and Achievement in Basic Education. http://www.girlseducation.org/PGE_Active_Pages/Resources/Publications/main .asp

Young, Mary Eming. 1996. *Early Child Development: Investing in the Future*. Washington, D.C.: World Bank.

———(ed.). 2001. *From Early Child Development to Human Development*. Washington, DC: World Bank.